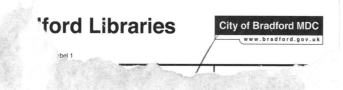

Developing Personal Safety Skills in Children with Disabilities

Developing Personal Safety Skills in Children with Disabilities

Freda Briggs

Jessica Kingsley Publishers
London and Philadelphia

Pages marked WORKSHEET may be photocopied

First published in the United Kingdom in 1995
by Jessica Kingsley Publishers
116 Pentonville Road
London N1 9JB, England
and
29 West 35th Street, 10th fl.
New York, NY 10001-2299, USA

www.jkp.com

Copyright © 1995 Freda Briggs
Illustrations copyright © 1995 Monica Love
Printed digitally since 2004

Library of Congress Cataloging in Publication Data
A CIP catalog record for this book is available from the Library of Congress

British Library Cataloguing in Publication Data
Briggs, Freda
Developing Personal Safety Skills in
Children with Disabilities
I. Title
371.9

ISBN 1 85302 245 4

Contents

Foreword   vii

Part 1:

1   All Children Need Personal Safety Skills   3

2   Why Children with Disabilities Need Personal Safety Programs   17

3   Parent Participation in Personal Safety Programs   29

4   Developing Curriculum: Suggestions for Developing Safety and Personal Development Curriculum for Children with Disabilities Using an Integrated Approach   49

5   Responding to the Actual or Suspected Sexual Abuse of Children   65

Part 2: Modules

Module 1   Developing Children's Self-Esteem   77

Module 2   Developing Children's Assertiveness Skills   90

Module 3   Coping with Hazards   96

Module 4   'It's My Body'   104

Module 5   Some Parts of our Bodies are Private   122

Module 6   Learning about our Feelings   138

Module 7   Talking About Touching   166

Appendix 1: Ways of Integrating Personal Safety into the Curriculum   200

Appendix 2: Other Reasons for the Protection of Children with Disabilities   201

Bibliography   203

Index   209

Foreword

Child protection has become a policy issue which most western governments have been forced to address. International research shows that children with disabilities are at greatest risk of all forms of maltreatment but services and the justice system focus on able-bodied, sighted and hearing children with average intelligence and sophisticated communication skills.

Canadian, British and American researchers have shown that the needs of children have been overlooked, first because these children are not acknowledged as a target population by the community at large and second, because service providers are so overwhelmed by problems that they have not begun to take up the challenge of addressing the special needs of this most vulnerable minority group.

This book was written at the specific request of teachers, social workers and psychologists who were seriously concerned about the lack of affordable materials for teaching safety skills to children with disabilities. They wanted a book which would provide the information needed by teachers and caregivers about child protection and disability. They also wanted a book which would provide curriculum ideas for teaching safety skills to children and young people with mild to severe disabilities in mainstreamed classes and special situations. At that time they were using a text written by the same author for adults working with children of normal intelligence in the 5–8-year age bracket. They found that the 'concepts were right' for working with older children with developmental disabilities but, of course, the illustrations were inappropriate.

The collection of curriculum ideas was contributed by child psychologist and sex educator Julie Smith and a team of experienced, practising special education teachers led by Enza del Vecchio, Fran Figeon and Alison Pickford, all of whom teach personal safety skills to children with physical and developmental disabilities. The manuscript was then submitted to Margaret Kennedy, Britain's pioneer in the protection of deaf children, Professor Dick Sobsey of the University of Alberta's Abuse and Disability Project and Dr. Jan Scown of Hamilton, New Zealand who in turn circulated the book to professionals involved in special education and requested feedback. Their suggestions were faithfully incorporated in the text.

From the outset, it was recognized that, to be effective, a child protection program must be open and honest, addressing some of the commonly experienced sexual behaviours which are encountered by children. These are, of course, the taboo subjects which adults tend to avoid. Teachers found that they were the only ones who felt uncomfortable when they first addressed these matters in an open and honest way. The children were at ease and helped the teachers' confidence to grow.

The curriculum ideas have been sequenced to help with the development of basic safety knowledge and skills. The author recognizes that they are generalist in nature and teachers will need to adapt them to suit individual needs. It is widely agreed that there is a need for teaching materials designed specifically for signing deaf children and blind children but it is beyond the scope of this volume to provide this high level of specialization.

Although it was our intention to create a book that would encourage teachers, parents and caregivers to teach safety skills to disabled children, the concepts, worksheets and ideas suggested in this book are equally appropriate for use with those who do not have disabilities.

Part 1

1 All Children Need Personal Safety Skills

The origins of education for child protection

Personal safety programs were introduced to schools in the United States in the mid 1970s in response to the alarming increase in reports of child sexual abuse, recognition of its damaging effects on victims and their families and the realization that the majority of cases involved not strangers, as had previously been thought, but adults who were known and trusted by their victims.

In 1973, American Rape Crisis Centres provided sexual abuse prevention talks for girls, focusing on how to avoid 'date rape' and assaults by strangers. In the same year, the Columbus (Ohio) Child Assault Prevention Project (CAPP) made a major breakthrough with the publication of a comprehensive protection program for adolescents.

The model which emerged from the radical feminist movement explained sexual abuse within the context of male power. This resulted in attempts to educate children about their rights and body ownership with the aim of empowering them to resist and report adults who behaved inappropriately.

In 1977, Cordelia Anderson, working at the Minneapolis County Attorney's Office, made another significant contribution with the introduction of the concept of the 'Touch Continuum' designed to help children to differentiate between good, bad and confusing touches, the last of which was intended to alert children to the risk of sexual contact. Anderson (1986), Plummer (1984, 1986), Tobin and Farley (1990) and other program authors expanded this concept to teach very young children about sexual abuse, hoping to reduce its occurrence.

In the meantime, the Royal Canadian Mounted Police recruited Surrey (British Columbia) School Board to review the available educational materials for child protection (1977). The trustees had reservations about their suitability and felt the need for a more comprehensive package to include community involvement. A non-profit making group was formed which became the Child Abuse Research and Education (CARE) Productions Association of BC. This group secured funding to employ a team of parents, teachers and teacher educators to produce and develop teaching resources for use in kindergartens and up to grade three. The CARE Kit was piloted in schools in British Columbia and Tacoma, Washington, USA in 1982.

It was subjected to systematic evaluation and revision and now, in the fifth edition, is used throughout the English speaking world.

In 1980, the US Government took a giant step forward when it provided grants to trial different methods of presenting personal safety information to school children to protect them from sexual abuse. By 1985, there were child protection programs in schools in all American states. In 1987, researchers Finkelhor and Strapko drew attention to the wide claims made relating to the effectiveness of school programs and the fact that very few had been subjected to independent evaluation with children. Designers were often social workers who, with little or no background in child development, presented child sexual abuse in a simplistic way from the adult female's perspective, underestimating the complexity of the concepts to be learned (Finkelhor and Strapko, 1987: Krivacska, 1990).

It was not until 1984 that the topic of child protection received serious attention in Australia and New Zealand, while the United Kingdom lagged far behind. Victoria Police (Australia) adopted an American 'anti-victimization' program, Protective Behaviours, which they promoted nation-wide in 1985. In the meantime, New Zealand Police and the Ministry of Education examined and rejected overseas programs and, at great expense, set out to create their own sensitive but 'open, honest and culturally and developmentally appropriate' national curriculum for use with all ages in all state schools. They seconded early childhood educators and curriculum designers to create teaching materials, pilot them in schools, evaluate children's progress and collate and examine the views of parents and teachers. The primary school modules of 'Keeping Ourselves Safe' were launched in 1987, subjected to independent evaluation in 1991 and revised to incorporate the research findings in 1994 (Briggs, 1991a, 1991b; Briggs and Hawkins, 1994b).

While schools in the United Kingdom have long accepted responsibility for teaching children to stay safe from fire, traffic and water, they have been slow to accept that children need to know how to stay safe with people. In 1986, Michelle Elliott's 'Kidscape' was introduced to provide 'Good sense defence' for five- to eleven-year-olds. Although it avoided controversy by concentrating on safety with bullies and dangerous strangers, there has been no widespread adoption of this or any other personal safety program. Neither sex education nor education for child protection have been incorporated into the National Curriculum for England and Wales. Adults' needs take precedence over children's rights and British professionals still have the option to choose whether to ignore or report evidence of child maltreatment.

What is most significant, however, is that all of the programs referred to were planned with physically active, intelligent children in mind; the protection of the most vulnerable group of children, those with disabilities, has been virtually ignored throughout the English-speaking world.

Why child protection programs are necessary

All children are vulnerable to sexual abuse

All children are at risk of sexual molestation regardless of their age, gender, race, ethnicity, social class or religious background. Most victims are abused by people they know. There are many reasons for children's vulnerability:

ALL CHILDREN ARE POWERLESS

They depend on adults to meet their basic needs. Sexual abuse involves the strong or better informed controlling and using the weak and uninformed for their own sexual gratification. Children are especially powerless when they are deprived of personal safety and sex education.

UNINFORMED CHILDREN TRUST ALL ADULTS

Five-year-olds are noted for their fearlessness while six- and seven-year-olds worry about monsters, ghosts, witches, night time shadows and being home alone. Without education for child protection, children under eight trust all adults who look or act in a kindly way. They view their parents as their sole protectors, even when their fathers are in prison for incest and domestic violence (Briggs, 1991a, 1991b; Briggs and Hawkins, 1993a). The most negligent parents take frightened children into their beds when they waken up in the night and feel afraid.

YOUNG CHILDREN ARE INCAPABLE OF ASSESSING ADULTS' MOTIVES

Child molesters use coercion, tricks, bribes, threats and blackmail to persuade children to do what they otherwise might not do. Piaget's theory of moral development (1965) tells us that children operating at a level of seven years or less are incapable of judging the motives of others. They assess people as good or bad not by their intentions but by their appearance, demeanour and the outcome of their actions. Child molesters are often perceived by victims as kind and trustworthy people because they show an interest in their victims or provide treats.

CHILDREN ARE TAUGHT THAT GOODNESS EQUATES WITH OBEDIENCE TO ADULTS

Without a child protection program, children believe that they have to obey all adults; this rule applies *even when they know that what the adult is doing or requesting is wrong* (Briggs, 1991a, 1991b). This enables adult offenders to offend with little risk of rejection. Children are especially vulnerable when they have been trained to suppress their own needs to please others.

CHILDREN ARE CURIOUS ABOUT THEIR OWN BODIES

Boys are particularly interested in genital matters because their sexuality is more public than that of girls. They start masturbating and acquire a sexual language at an early age. Their 'private parts' are anything but private; they handle them in public toilets several times a day and have the facility to compare size and shape. They are sexually aroused by looking at other boys' erections and sexual interactions result. Because of cultural taboos, sexualized peer groups have the attractive qualities of secret societies which boys enjoy (Cook and Howells, 1981). Membership of such groups substantially increases vulnerability to abuse by adolescent and adult predators. Paedophiles commonly stimulate boys' curiosity by introducing sex talk and pornography in the guise of providing sex education which their parents neglected (Briggs, 1995).

CHILDREN ARE DEPRIVED OF BASIC INFORMATION ABOUT THEIR SEXUALITY

Children are sexual beings. In western society, four letter words are now commonplace, pornography is widely available, homosexuality and cases of rape are discussed in news reports and documentaries and films bring naked strangers simulating sexual intercourse into children's homes. Parents ignore all of this and pretend that children hear nothing, see nothing and learn nothing about sexual matters. Traditional parenting styles create a taboo on sexual matters, denying children's sexuality in the hope that denial will keep children ignorant (often referred to as 'innocent') and asexual. There is a widespread (mistaken) assumption that knowledge will result in experimentation although international research shows that it is ignorance and the lack of information that leads to unsafe sex and unwanted pregnancies (Goldman and Goldman, 1988).

Wurtele (1993) found that American parents only gave children vocabulary for the 'private' parts of the body *after* they had become involved in child protection programs. Without such programs, if parents refer to them at all, they use euphemisms. Because girls' genitals are hidden, most parents use the word 'down there' or 'bottom' to refer to the entire buttock–anal–genital area. As a consequence, girls seldom know how may orifices they have until they are old enough to use a hand mirror.

Boys are taught to use 'pet' or ethnic names for penis in the hope that no one will understand them if they refer to it in public. In a group of six-year-old boys, the author discovered 20 different words for 'penis'. They ranged from names such as 'John Henry', 'John Thomas', 'Dick' and 'Willy' to 'pee pee', 'wee wee', 'cock', 'prick', 'thing', 'worm' and even 'grub'. The most unusual was 'golf set', explained as 'a stick, two balls and a bag'. The boy's parents thought this highly amusing until it was pointed out that no adult outside the immediate family would be able to help their son if he had occasion to complain that someone had misbehaved with his 'golf set'.

The message transmitted to children is that they can talk about their eyelids, ear lobes, nostrils and any other body part, but their genitals must remain invisible and unmentionable in the presence of adults. Children recognize the hypocrisy when parents and teachers say, 'You can talk to me if something is worrying you' when, by their very avoidance of the subject, adults demonstrate that they cannot cope with information about the lower half of the human body. Children of five and six know that adults 'blow a fuse', 'get mad', 'throw a fit' or 'go bananas' when children talk about or do anything remotely sexual. They also know that adults have double standards: they like doing 'sexy' things, looking at 'sexy' pictures and watching 'sexy' films. When asked, 'Why do you think adults get so mad with kids?', some five- to six-year-old Australian and New Zealanders replied, 'Adults like sex but they don't want kids doing it. They just want to keep it all to themselves' (Briggs, 1991a, 1991b).

Unfortunately, parent–child communications do not improve as children grow older. In recent Australian studies, 88 per cent of parents of 16-year-olds claimed that they were 'open to discussion' on sexual matters; 89 per cent claimed to have discussed safe sex and sexually transmitted diseases with their offspring. Interviews with the children showed that these claims were untrue.

A second study of 1800 adolescents and their parents confirmed that 81 per cent had never talked to their fathers and 69 per cent had never talked to their mothers about sexual matters. The topic of safe sex, homosexuality (which is of particular concern to male abuse victims and participants in male peergroup sex), and AIDS were taboo subjects in most homes. When left to schools, sex education tends to come too late and it concentrates on reproduction.

Professor Doreen Rosenthal of Melbourne's La Trobe University confirmed that while parents in the 1990s have a 'rosy glow' about their role as sex educators, they are deluding themselves (Weekes and Westwood 1993).

Children are highly sensitive to adults' taboos. They are unlikely to disclose sexual misbehaviour to parents or teachers unless they know, with absolute certainty, that the adults can handle information of a sexual nature without reacting emotionally. They are least likely to report sexual abuse when they view their parents as unapproachable.

Educators now recognise the dangers of putting adults' needs before children's needs; Hindman summed up this situation succinctly:

> The avoidance of genitalia may work well for adults who are uncomfortable discussing anything sexual with children but it harms children and prevention efforts by sending a mystical and confusing message to kids. On one hand we want to open communication lines with children and encourage reporting of sexual abuse. Yet, at the same time, by avoiding a discussion of genitalia we demonstrate our inability to talk about even the simplest aspects of sexuality to children. The message is that we can't say these words but they should be sure and come and tell us if someone touches those "parts", "stuff", "deals down there". (Mayes *et al.*, 1992, p.45)

UNINFORMED CHILDREN DO NOT REALIZE THAT ABUSIVE BEHAVIOUR IS WRONG

If young and developmentally disabled children have not been taught the limits of acceptable and unacceptable behaviour, they usually regard sexual abuse as 'normal'. This is especially likely when offences involve older children, siblings or caregivers. Male adult survivors told the author that while they knew that 'sex' was a taboo, their childhood definition of sex involved men and women and 'making babies' which 'had nothing at all to do with what was happening' to them in all male environments such as school dormitories, sports changing rooms, scout meetings and camps and even their own bedrooms (Briggs, 1995). Young children are least likely to recognize genital fondling as wrong if they find it pleasurable (Cook and Howells, 1981).

SEXUAL ABUSE IS OFTEN PRESENTED AS EVIDENCE OF AFFECTION

Children who have had no safety education often accept the perpetrator's explanation that sexual abuse is what people normally do when they love each other. Paedophiles seek out children who look sad, lonely and affection starved. They are noted for their capacity to tap into children's emotional needs. They find professional and voluntary work in children's services. They seek out single mothers for attention to gain access to their families. They derive satisfaction from every stage of the seduction process, devoting a great deal of time to potential victims, listening to them, inviting their confidence, boosting their egos and developing their trust and the trust of their parents. Victims then tolerate the most painful abuse as the price they have to pay for the relationship (Briggs, 1995).

CHILDREN ARE EVEN AT RISK IN THEIR PEER GROUPS

Parents who are unaware of the dynamics of child molestation transport their children to and from child care centres, schools, clubs and other group situations, convinced that, by being taxi drivers, they are doing all that is necessary to keep their children safe. It seldom occurs to parents that children might be unsafe in groups.

Boys are particularly vulnerable to seduction in all male peer groups. It is comparatively easy for a paedophile to overcome the resistance of an uninformed child if he can show that what is happening is 'normal'. Reluctant and hesitant children are persuaded that they are the odd ones out: 'What's wrong with you?...Look, it's fun. Everyone else does it. I promise you'll like it.'

Offenders tap into boy's fears of being perceived as different. Large groups of children featured in allegations against Christian Brothers in Canada, the United States and Australia. In May 1994 a Christian Brother was charged with 72 offences involving group sex with 35 Aboriginal children on beaches and other public places on remote Bathurst Island in the Timor Sea.

Clearly, no one can be trusted by virtue of their occupation, relationship or even gender. On the other hand, we cannot teach children to fear all adults. That is why we have a duty to provide personal safety education which will help children to identify, avoid and report inappropriate behaviour.

CHILDREN ARE CONFUSED BY SEXUAL MISBEHAVIOUR

Because parents reprimand young children for showing their genitals in public and using 'dirty talk', they (and girls in particular) are shocked and confused by their first encounter with a sexually aroused adult. While the offender may give assurances that nothing is wrong, the behaviour indicates otherwise. Offenders take advantage of victims' confusion to gain their compliance.

Unless children have the knowledge and confidence to recognize, stop, escape from and report the first sexual contact and unless they know from experience that adults can be trusted to protect them without blaming, offences continue, increasing in frequence and violence.

CHILDREN ARE SELDOM ENCOURAGED TO EXPRESS THEIR ANXIETIES AND FEARS

With the best of intentions, parents reassure children that there is nothing to worry about (when they're petrified) and 'it doesn't hurt' (when they're in agony). Most boys feel that they have to be self-reliant, brave and strong. The western concept of masculinity is the antithesis of victimization. Male victims are unlikely to report abuse if they fear that they were singled out because of their homosexual characteristics or, alternatively, they are aware of the stigma associated with homosexuality (Briggs, 1995; Briggs and Hawkins, 1994a; Cook and Howells, 1981; Hunter, 1990). Girls are trapped by the fear that, if they report intrafamilial abuse, their families will break up and they will be held responsible.

Without personal safety programs, young children are vulnerable to dangerous strangers

Although most children are taught to avoid dangerous strangers, the testing of 378 Australian and New Zealand children (aged 5–8 years) before and after exposure to a national school-based safety program confirmed that children who lack personal safety education are vulnerable to abduction by strangers because they believe that:

- they can trust all adults except strangers
- they have never seen a stranger but would recognize one instantly if they saw one
- strangers are always males who are readily identifiable by their evil appearance, black clothing, masks, evil eyes and the way in which they leer at children
- adults who look and seem kind *are* kind
- women are never strangers and they can always be trusted to help children

- teachers would never allow strangers to enter school premises.

So strong is the stereotyping of the evil male stranger that class after class of five-to eight-year-olds told the author (who had just arrived on an international flight) that they had never seen a stranger in their lives. They were adamant that the author was not a stranger because 'she looks nice...like my grandma', 'sounds nice' and 'she's got a briefcase, which means she works...and strangers never work...they just rob and steal kids'. Children defined a stranger as a half human, half monster who wears a mask, breaks into houses, kidnaps children from their beds, snatches them on their way to and from school and kills them. The children acquired this information from parents, peers, news reports, programs about wanted criminals and even TV advertisements (Briggs, 1991a, 1991b; Briggs and Hawkins, 1993b).

Fearing only these imaginary creatures, 75 per cent of five- to six-year-olds and 50 per cent of seven-year-olds assured the researchers that, if they became lost in crowded places, they would look for and accept an offer of help from any adult with a smiling, kindly face who offered to take them home or reunite them with their missing parents. They would not tell shop personnel of their plight because 'shop people don't know where I live...it isn't their job to take kids home...they couldn't leave their work...and they might take me to a stranger'. Children would not tell police on duty at pageants, sports events or street parades that they were lost because 'Police have important work to do... They arrest robbers and take them to jail... They don't have time to take kids home... And they'd tell me off for getting lost'. Although these children knew that police and shop assistants have access to telephones, radios and public address systems, they did not think that they could be used to help them. The only safe suggestions came from children who, while visiting a new Woolworths store with their teacher, had been given a practical demonstration of how lost children are helped to find their parents.

In the meantime, whole classes of five- and six-year-olds would accompany any unknown woman who met them outside school and claimed that 'Mummy can't come...she's sick'. They rationalized that adults tell the truth, that the person was being kind and, furthermore, that someone who knows their name or claims to know their parents must be a friend. Interestingly, none of the children would have returned to school to tell a teacher because, apart from the fact that schools are 'spooky' when children leave, they perceived the teachers' authority as limited to the class and the classroom.

It became very clear that, while children had been indoctrinated with the fear of dangerous strangers, their very concept of 'stranger' was so defective that they would accompany the first kind looking adult who offered to help them while ignoring the safest resources.

Without education for personal safety, children keep sexual behaviour secret

Child sexual abuse thrives on secrecy. Most children have been reprimanded or threatened with punishment for telling family secrets. Many a child who tries to share a secret about abuse is assured by a gullible parent or teacher that 'we all have to keep secrets'.

Without protective education, children think that they must remain silent about sexual misbehaviour. They believe that they would be punished several times: first, for breaking the secrecy: second, because reporting would involve 'rude' or 'dirty talk' which is viewed as a punishable offence and, third, because the bad behaviour occurred (even if they said 'No' and escaped). Finally, children believed that their parents would tell the perpetrator that they had told his or her secret, resulting in further punishment. Because they viewed the crime of breaking an adult's secret as more serious than the crime of initiating sexual misbehaviour, they believed that their mothers would support the offender, rather than them (Briggs, 1991a, 1991b). The propensity for secrecy increases with the age of the child (Watson and Valtin, 1993).

Multi-cultural Australian and New Zealand children believed that all sexual behaviour must be kept secret because 'it's naughty' and it 'makes adults very cross'. Naughty means that 'you're bad and nobody will love you…you deserve to be punished…it's your own fault'.

An additional trap for children of seven plus years is the belief that they could not disclose sexual misbehaviour to parents or teachers because 'your brothers or sisters or other kids would find out. They'd tease you and you'd feel embarrassed and they'd say, "He (she) must be stupid to have done those yukky things"'.

Psychologists have long been concerned that adult survivors blame themselves for abuse in childhood. The Australian and New Zealand research showed that the blame-the-victim stance was well established in very young children. Without child protection programs which address these issues, children believe that, 'if someone does bad things to you, it must be your own fault; you must have done something to deserve it' (Briggs, 1991a, 1991b).

Without parent involvement in education for child protection, children do not trust their parents to protect them from unwanted touching

Prior to involvement in a school program, all of the 378 Australian and New Zealand children interviewed by the author revealed that they had, at some time, asked relatives to desist from sloppy kissing, excessive tickling, squeezing and rough play. All of the children said that their pleas were ignored; 20 per cent said that they could not trust their parents to protect them from other adults. Typically, parents defended the perpetrators and derided the children for complaining. Asian and Pacific Island children believed that their parents were powerless to protect them from older relatives with higher status in the family hierarchy.

Before participation in a school-based child protection program, most parents urged their children to tolerate unwanted and uncomfortable touching to please adults. When boys and girls objected to sloppy, wet mouth kisses from aged female relatives, scratchy hugs and unshaven uncles and pipe-smoking grandfathers who smelt like garden incinerators, they were all reprimanded for being inconsiderate.

'Grandad will be upset if you don't let him kiss you'.

'Don't be a cry baby… It doesn't hurt… He's only teasing'.

Boys who complained of sloppy wet kisses and too tight hugs from female relatives received the same kind of admonition.

Children of five to eight years were alarmingly cynical about adults' priorities. 'Grown ups stick together', they said. 'They don't believe kids. When we tell them an adult has done bad things, they say "You're making it up"'.

When parents fail to support children's attempts at assertiveness, they give the very strong message that children's feelings are unimportant. It is this sense of low self-worth and powerlessness which facilitates victimization. A seven-year-old New Zealander in a school with no child protection curriculum summed up the situation as follows:

OK, I may have the right to say, "No" to bad touching but what's the use? It doesn't do any good when you're talking to grown ups. Sometimes it makes things much worse. When I ask them to stop, they think it's funny and do it all the more. I've decided that it's better to say nothing and just put up with it.

By contrast, when parents participated in programs, they were more likely to protect their children's interests, explaining to relatives that their grandchildren or nephews still loved them but no longer wanted to be kissed. They acknowledged children's feelings and helped them to assert themselves, increasing their confidence and trust.

Sexual abuse is damaging to children's development

Unfortunately, early sexualization damages children's development irrespective of whether victims like or dislike the abuser's behaviour. Some abused children become obsessed with sexual matters and their overtly sexualized behaviour is then recognized by other offenders, increasing the risk of multiple and more violent abuse. Victimization then becomes a way of life. Sexually obsessed children re-enact the abuse with peers and younger children, using the same seduction techniques that they experienced. They perpetuate the abuse cycle, creating another generation of victims and offenders. Boys who have been abused by males are most likely to abuse other boys and those abused by females are likely to abuse girls. Children victimized by both male and female offenders are likely to abuse both boys and girls (Briggs and Hawkins, 1994a). Victims who have learned that sex pleases adults may behave sexually with teachers or older children of the same gender as their abusers. Uninformed staff usually label them as promiscuous.

Victims who enjoyed abusive activity in their early years often suffer enormous guilt, self-recrimination and anger when, with maturity, they realize that they were 'used' and deceived. There is a high correlation between sexual abuse and later self-abuse with drugs, alcoholism and attempted suicides.

Most survivors suffer from low self-esteem and find it difficult to trust and relate to other people. Male survivors often feel that they live in a sexual void, not trusting men (if they suffered homosexual abuse) yet unable to respond to the emotional needs of women. Both male and female survivors may experience mental and physical ill health and unemployment (Bagley and King, 1990; Briggs, 1995; Briggs and Hawkins, 1994a; MacFarlane and Waterman, 1986).

What children need to know to stay safe

The aim of personal safety education is to give children enough information to be able to respond safely to an abusive situation before it becomes serious. This does not make children responsible for protecting themselves (Adams, 1986). Failure to reaffirm this could result in victims feeling responsible for their own victimization (Mayes *et al.*, 1992).

To stay safe children need to be able to:

- respect their own bodies and the bodies of others
- identity potentially unsafe situations and take steps to stay safe

- avoid and report older children and adults who introduce 'dirty' talk, 'dirty' photos, magazines and videos (given that these commonly precede severe forms of abuse)

- recognize and reject secrets, tricks, bribes and blackmail and threats involving sexual misbehaviour

- recognize, escape from and report sexual misbehaviour, irrespective of the relationship of the perpetrator to the child

- get help in an emergency, tell reliable adults and keep on telling until safety is restored.

These skills involve very complex learning processes, the rules of which often conflict with what parents teach their children. There is, of course, no assurance that children will use their knowledge and skills when the need arises. We must never underestimate the power that adults wield and the attractiveness of the baits used by paedophiles. International studies confirm, however, that children are most vulnerable when they are ignorant of their rights and lack information about what constitutes unacceptable behaviour (Finkelhor, 1984).

Children involved in child protection programs are less likely to be victimized than uninformed children

Recent interviews with 100 multi-cultural child molesters showed that they chose ignorant and powerless victims and avoided confident, knowledgeable children. Furthermore, when victims of father–daughter incest became involved in school programs and challenged their fathers, some men told their children to 'do the right thing and report it' (Briggs and Hawkins, 1994a). They confirmed Budin and Johnson's findings that children who have participated in safety programs are much less likely to be selected for victimization than those who have no knowledge of their rights (1989).

What constitutes an effective program?

One of the most frequently used methods of judging the effectiveness of a child protection curriculum is to assess changes in children's knowledge before and after exposure to school sessions. Can they remember what was taught? More important, can they transfer the knowledge to different but related situations?

Studies show that children who have been exposed to even the shortest programs gain some safety knowledge. However, the most successful programs are those which:

- involve parents at every stage so that they can reinforce concepts at home and provide opportunities to practise problem solving and the application of new skills

- provide a combination of concrete activities for children

- involve audio-visual teaching materials to reinforce learning

- incorporate concepts which are appropriate for the children's developmental levels;

Studies show that the best combination for learning is a mixture of information, role plays, puppets and opportunities to learn and practise safety skills (Wurtele *et al.*, 1986). Teaching must be open and honest, using children's own language so that they can clearly understand what is OK and not OK (Conte, Rosen, Saperstein and Shermack, 1985; Downer, 1984; Gilbert *et al.* 1989, Mayes *et al.* 1990; Saslawsky and Wurtele, 1986). Young and developmentally disabled children are the ones least likely to understand vague hints or concepts and transfer them to complex abusive situations; for example, children seldom relate rules about 'unsafe' or 'unwanted *touching*' to oral sex which does not involve the use of their hands.

In a survey of 25 American programs, Finkelhor and Strapko (1987) confirmed that the most effective were the most comprehensive programs of the longest duration with the maximum involvement of children and frequent opportunities for reinforcement. The least effective were those which relied on abstract concepts.

In a comparison of the effectiveness of the (Wisconsin) Protective Behaviours Program (used in Australia) and the New Zealand's 'Keeping Ourselves Safe', it was found that all children made improvements in problem-solving skills in the intial stages but the New Zealand children had significantly higher scores one year later (Briggs, 1991a, 1991b; Briggs and Hawkins, 1994b). While the New Zealand curriculum was timetabled throughout the school and teaching materials were provided, the empowerment model was viewed more as a 'way of life' to be used as a teaching strategy. Teaching was spasmodic and selective with most teachers. Most Australian teachers omitted the crucial, sensitive aspects of the adult:child power differential, the circumstances in which a child can say 'No' to adults and matters relating to adults' secrets and sexual misbehaviour. Australian parents were lulled into a false sense of security because while they thought that their children were being taught all that they needed to know to stay safe, their children thought that Protective Behaviours strategies only applied to their relationships with peers on school premises and that they must continue to obey all adults, keep their secrets and tolerate unwanted touching.

In the most successful school programs, parents are involved throughout the program, receiving weekly communications relating to what has been taught and how they can evaluate and reinforce children's learning. By that means, personal safety strategies can be adopted as a way of life. In the New Zealand study, the factor which influenced children's gains in safety knowledge was not their age, gender, intelligence level or race but whether or not their parents showed an interest in their safety and reinforced the program's concepts at home.

For many years, pessimists have devalued school-based child protection programs because no concrete evidence was available to show that children used the strategies taught when they encountered real life victimization. The pessimism can now be challenged thanks to the 1993 research findings of David Finkelhor and colleagues at the University of New Hampshire. They show conclusively that children use the learned safety strategies to stop and report victimization. Funded by Boy Scouts of America, the researchers interviewed 2000 children and their parents in 440 different school districts. Sixty-seven per cent of participants had been involved in personal safety education and those in the most comprehensive programs had the highest scores on safety knowledge. The researchers investigated children's experiences of victimization in the preceding year and found that 25 per cent of children had used the strategies to protect themselves and an additional 25 per cent had used them to protect their friends. The high scorers on safety knowledge were the ones most likely to have acted safely, reported the incidents and felt positive about their efforts. The researchers found that while school programs did not necessarily prevent victimization, they helped to reduce the severity and increased the level of reporting.

Comprehensive parental instruction and participation made the significant difference to children's coping skills and knowledge. Parent participation also resulted in children limiting the seriousness of abuse and reporting it. Well-informed parents are usually the most approachable and the ones most likely to handle reports in psychologically helpful ways.

Without education for child protection, few adults know how to keep children safe

Without the benefit of child protection programs, parents do not know how to teach children to stay safe (Berrick, 1988). They underestimate the damage caused by sexual abuse and they have unrealistic notions relating to both the signs of abuse and the characteristics of offenders. In American studies cited by Mayes *et al.* (1992), 5 per cent of parents believed that abuse happened because children 'act in a sexy way' and the remainder believed offenders were 'mentally ill'. Parents consoled themselves that their children were safe it there was no history of psychiatric illness in the family.

Parent surveys show that only 29 per cent of American and 25 per cent of Australian parents told their children anything about personal safety and, in both countries, they merely warned children to avoid being kidnapped by male strangers in cars (Briggs, 1987; Finkelhor, 1981, Mayes *et al.* 1992). They postponed giving information until 'next year' or 'when they're older' or 'I'll tell them when they ask about it'. It is, of course, unrealistic to expect children to ask questions relating to such matters when parents are so obviously incapable of dealing with them. Both in the USA and Australia, children were deemed to be 'too young' for protective education regardless of their age.

Without child protection programs which develop reporting skills, child victims only give hints about abuse

Many victims believe that their parents already know what is happening to them, either because the offender said, 'Don't bother to tell your mother about this. She knows what I'm doing. She says it's OK.' or because parents give the impression that they are all-seeing, all-knowing and omnipotent. When mothers say, 'I know what you're thinking', young children believe them.

An additional complication is that victims use the offender's language and the child's perspective of what happened. As a consequence, children think that they are reporting inappropriate behaviour when they make statements such as:

'I don't like the taste of his ice cream';

'He has a magic stick';

'I don't like--------. He's mean/she's mean/He's gross/she's gross';

'I don't like the way he tickles me';

'Mummy, is it alright for-------to do funny things?'

'I've got a secret I can't tell';

'I don't like the games he plays';

'He wears funny underpants'.

And whereas children who have not been taught reporting skills believe that these statements constitute cries for help, their unprepared parents and teachers ignore them or respond with statements such as,

'We have to keep secrets';

'We all have to learn to put up with teasing';

'He plays games because he likes you';

'It's great if he's funny and makes you laugh'.

By comparison, a parent or teacher who has been involved in protective education is more likely to ask questions such as,

'Where do you see him in his underpants?';

'Show me where he tickles you';

'How do you play that game? Who plays with you?';

'What will happen if you tell the secret? Who says so? Who else knows the secret?'.

These basic questions enable caring adults to assess the seriousness of the problem and discuss strategies for stopping unwanted behaviour of all kinds.

Without the confidence and knowledge that comes from a comprehensive safety program, children will not risk telling their terrible secrets to the most caring of parents because they fear that love will be withdrawn. Children know that their mothers will be upset. This fear is realistic when the perpetrator is the mother's sexual partner (Briggs, 1991a; Briggs and Hawkins 1994a and 1994b).

Without education for child protection, adults fail to recognize victims' cries for help

Berrick (1988) found that, without involvement in child protection programs, parents have no idea what to look for when sexual abuse is suspected. Unless parents and professionals have a sound knowledge of children's reactions to child sexual abuse, they dismiss the signs and symptoms as a 'passing phase' in normal child development. All too frequently, victims are labelled as 'emotionally disturbed' children with behavioural and learning problems and the cause of their problems is never investigated. Most teachers and care givers look for everyday explanations for the changes that occur to children's personalities and emotional wellbeing following victimization. Child sexual abuse is only considered as a possibility when other options have all been investigated and found wanting. With the benefit of hindsight, parents and teachers often realize that victims gave many different clues over a prolonged period of time before sexual abuse was identified. And even when cries for help are explicit, without specific education, neither parents nor professionals are likely to handle disclosures in psychologically helpful ways. The recipients of information are usually embarrassed or accuse victims of lying or misinterpreting normal affectionate behaviour. They either ignore what was said or absolve themselves of responsibility by telling the perpetrator of the allegation. This ensures that victims are punished for making disclosures, threats increase and the abuse continues. When trusted adults are unsupportive, children accept the victim role, assuming that they are helpless, hopeless and not worth helping.

Without education for child protection, signs of sexual abuse are often mistaken for the signs of normal sexual curiosity

Without education for child protection, parents and professionals confuse normal sexual curiosity and the signs of abuse. The offender then gets the benefit of the doubt and the opportunity to re-offend. Children are interested in the construction of their bodies and this curiosity increases when they become aware of gender differences. Children's normal curiosity involves touching their own genitals or asking to look at or touch other people's genitals. Participants have equal rights on the lines of, 'You show me yours and I'll show you mine'.

Teachers, child care personnel and parents sometimes encounter young children behaving sexually with younger children. Their problem is to decide whether the behaviour constitutes normal curiosity or whether it is a sign that one or more of the participants is re-enacting sexual abuse. In general, sexual abuse is likely to be the cause when there is a substantial difference in the age, power, size or knowledge of the children and when one or more participants use threats, bribes, coercion, blackmail, force, tricks or secrecy to gain the cooperation of a victim. We should always consider the possibility that the initiators are victims of sexual abuse when they demand sexual acts and use language associated with adults and pornography; for example, when children invite others to kiss or suck their genitals, when they insert objects into vaginal or anal openings or they enquire whether others like it when they engage in genital fondling. When young children are obsessed with sexual matters in their drawings, their play with dolls and their conversation, there is a strong possibility that they have been sexualized prematurely. And neither oral nor anal sex are features of children's normal curiosity.

All too frequently, professionals ignore children who are obsessed with sex talk and sexual behaviour. They assume that the children see their parents' sexual activities or watch pornographic videos at home. Unfortunately, many children *are* exposed to pornography. This is a form of sexual abuse and should be reported. Parents who watch porn often justify their actions on the basis that their children are 'too young to understand'. They should be reminded that children are constantly learning and when they see pornography they are learning about distorted sex roles. Girls learn that it's all right to be whipped, tied to a bed and raped and boys learn that men do it and women enjoy it. It should also be remembered that offenders commonly use pornography to arouse children's curiosity and persuade them to act out what they see.

Unfortunately, there is no 'quick fix' for the problem of child sexual abuse. Safety skills cannot be taught by exposing children to a single session or even a series of sessions of information. Teaching must be ongoing, reinforced by sound adult models and opportunities for children to practise skills. In the most effective programs, safety methods are adopted in teaching strategies for classroom management and they are integrated across school curriculum. When caregivers have been negligent or over-protective, support and positive reinforcement will be necessary to achieve changes.

2 Why Children with Disabilities Need Personal Safety Programs

Children with disabilities are the children at greatest risk of sexual abuse

American and Canadian studies suggest that children with disabilities are from three to seven times more likely to experience sexual abuse than non disabled children. Senn (1988) summarizes a number of studies which suggest that up to 69 per cent of girls and 30 per cent of boys with developmental disabilities are sexually abused before the age of 18. In a Seattle study, it was found that up to 500 disabled children a year were sexually abused in that city alone. Only 20 per cent of cases were reported and 99 per cent of offenders were known and trusted by their victims (Watson, 1984). These disclosures shocked the community. Many people took it for granted that children with disabilities were 'immune' from sexual abuse because they were perceived as 'sexually unattractive' by popular standards. Others knew of the risks and ignored them, either because they felt that the problem was too difficult or because they thought, mistakenly, that children with disabilities were already damaged and unlikely to be harmed by something that they could not fully understand (Watson, 1984).

Children with developmental disabilities are at highest risk of sexual abuse. Susan Hard (1986, cited in Senn, 1988, p.5) showed that 68 per cent of intellectually disabled girls were victimized before the age of 18 years. Chamberlain *et al.* (1984, cited in Senn 1988, p.4) found that 25 per cent of adolescent girls with intellectual disabilities had experienced rape or attempted rape. One third of the perpetrators were their fathers or father figures.

The incidence of sexual abuse involving deaf and non verbal children is also significantly higher than in the non disabled population. British and American research shows that:

- more than half of all deaf boys are sexually abused
- boys are more at risk than girls
- deaf children are at greater risk in residential schools than at home
- 25 per cent are abused in both home and school environments

- 80 per cent to 100 per cent of all deaf children in programs for the emotionally disturbed are there *because* of the effects of sexual abuse

- victims rarely receive therapeutic support for handling the emotionally damaging aspects of their experiences (Kennedy, 1989; Mounty and Fetterman, 1989; Sullivan, Vernon and Scanlon, 1987).

Despite the very high risks, scant attention is given to the protection of children with disabilities.

Children with severe disabilities often have restricted social environments

The social environment of the child with severe disabilities is usually more limited than the environment of non disabled children. When children use special transport to attend special schools or centres with a strong medical or technological focus, they lack opportunities to develop normal peer relationships. Their lives often conform to strict routines devised by their teachers, caregivers, therapists and medical personnel. They become adult orientated and desensitized to the norms of adult behaviour outside institutional settings. It is then more difficult for children to discriminate between appropriate and inappropriate touching. Lacking opportunities for independence, they miss the daily opportunities for problem solving, decision making and confidence building that are available to non disabled children.

An additional hazard is that adult caregivers often permit different standards of behaviour and adopt different expectations in their relationships with disabled children, unwittingly increasing their vulnerability to abuse. Children with intellectual disabilities are often permitted or even encouraged to be indiscriminately affectionate with strangers who visit their homes and schools.

Because of this, disabled children are viewed as ideal victims by sexual predators. Magazines produced by American paedophile clubs advised readers to select children affected by Down Syndrome, first because they are conspicuous, second because they are regarded as affectionate and eager to please and third, they are 'safe' targets because if they complain, police are reluctant to prosecute and put intellectually disabled children in the witness box (Husler, cited in Sank and La Fleche, 1981; Shuker, cited in Longo and Gochenour, 1981).

Children with severe disabilities are powerless

Wurtele (1987) found that the child's ability to exercise power relates to the need for acceptance; the greater the need for acceptance, the less able the child is to exercise power. Children with disabilities are the ones most likely to suffer from low self-esteem, feelings of isolation and powerlessness (Kennedy, 1991).

Children who depend on others for their basic needs are 'trained to be obedient, polite, nice to adults and to do what they're told' (Senn, 1988). They must conform to therapy requirements and be compliant to receive life support treatment. The power difference between adults and children increases when children are intellectually disadvantaged, deaf, non verbal, emotionally deprived or dependent on adults for their basic daily needs. Compliance and powerlessness increase with a reduction in communication skills.

Loss of personal freedom results in passivity and passivity, in turn, increases vulnerability to sexual abuse. In other words, good, compliant children are the most vulnerable to victimization.

Children with disabilities are disadvantaged by the volume and nature of their 'touch' contact

Children with disabilities are handled by many more adults than non disabled children. They may also be dependent on others for their personal hygiene and basic care.

Due to the integral role that caregivers play in children's lives, strong emotional attachments are often formed. These are helpful in most cases but the level of vulnerability to sexual abuse increases with the prolongation of dependency and the number of caregivers involved (Senn, 1988).

Staffing arrangements in residential settings often place children and caregivers in embarrassing and risky situations. Night attendants are often males, even when they have responsibility for attending to the most intimate needs of female adolescents. Male adolescents are often cared for by female staff during the day. This can be particularly embarrassing for boys incapacitated as a result of a recent diving or road accident, prior to which they attended to their own hygiene and toileting needs. Female staff try to hide their discomfort by joking about boys' genitals, especially when they have erections.

Staffing schedules often deprive staff and residents from having a choice in who provides personal care. This increases the powerlessness of children and creates unnecessary risks for clients and caregivers.

Implicit in these staffing arrangements is the assumption that adolescents with disabilities are insensitive to situations that would embarrass other people or, alternatively, that their feelings are of no importance. When staff protest, managers with a medical background sometimes defend their arrangements on the basis that hospitals employ male and female nurses to care for patients of either sex. Such arguments are unacceptable, first because adolescents with disabilities are not sick; second, the residential institution is their home, not a hospital; third, we cannot assume that hospital patients are not embarrassed by their inability to attend to their toileting needs; most are never asked.

The following diagrams show how children with severe physical disabilities are disadvantaged in terms of their sexual touch. They also demonstrate the importance of involving children's families and all school personnel in personal safety programs.

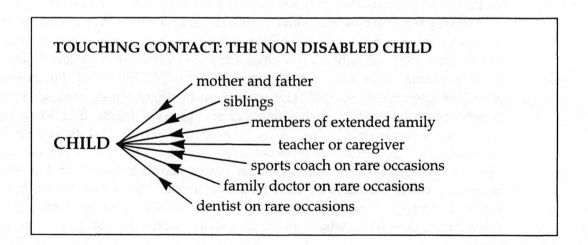

TOUCHING CONTACT: THE NON DISABLED CHILD

CHILD
- mother and father
- siblings
- members of extended family
- teacher or caregiver
- sports coach on rare occasions
- family doctor on rare occasions
- dentist on rare occasions

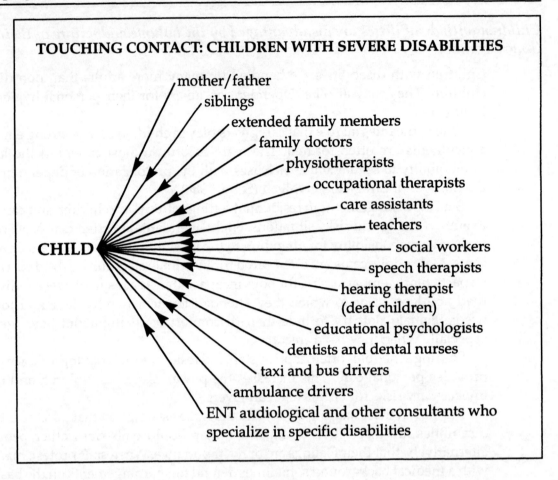

TOUCHING CONTACT: CHILDREN WITH SEVERE DISABILITIES

mother/father
siblings
extended family members
family doctors
physiotherapists
occupational therapists
care assistants
teachers
social workers
speech therapists
hearing therapist
(deaf children)
educational psychologists
dentists and dental nurses
taxi and bus drivers
ambulance drivers
ENT audiological and other consultants who
specialize in specific disabilities

CHILD

Garbarino *et al.* (1987) confirm that, when children with disabilities are sexually abused, the perpetrators are often the people responsible for the most intimate aspects of their day to day care.

Sobsey (1994) also shows that, in the analysis of 215 cases in the University of Alberta Abuse and Disability project, 67 per cent of all offenders contacted their victims through special services for the disabled and more than half of the offenders were paid staff or volunteers providing a service relating to the victims' disabilities. There is also a high risk of abuse by older peers with disabilities encountered through special services. Sobsey concluded that, '... much of the excess risk of abuse for people with disabilities may result from their exposure to the service system'.

The very fact that children with disabilities are most frequently abused by their caregivers makes it extremely difficult for them to prevent or report offences (Conte and Berliner, 1981; Finkelhor, 1979, 1986). They are least likely to protest if they risk the loss of vital links with major care providers (PACER, 1986). Furthermore, offenders often create special relationships to facilitate abuse, making victims dependent upon them for their emotional and physical needs. If children resist sexual advances, their resistance may be broken down by threats to withdraw essential care. Such threats are especially effective when children feel unwanted or rejected. Children are also confused when trusted people assure them that what is happening constitutes normal, affectionate behaviour: 'You know I wouldn't ask you to do something wrong. I'm the one who looks after you, remember. And it doesn't hurt, does it? So what's all the fuss about? Come on, you know you really like it.'

Not surprisingly, Sobsey found that only 14 per cent of cases involving disabled children were reported, fewer than 8 per cent of offenders were charged and only 8 per cent of those were acquitted (Sobsey, 1994).

Because offenders take advantage of children's confusion, it is especially important that children with disabilities are taught how to differentiate between acceptable and unacceptable touching and how to reject and report the unacceptable. However, we must never underestimate the difficulties that children have in exercising their rights when offenders are adult caregivers.

Children with disabilities are deprived of sex education

It is now widely accepted that, to protect all children from the risk of sexual abuse, age appropriate sex education must be offered alongside personal safety programs (Krivacska, 1990). This is especially important for reducing the incidence of abuse involving children with developmental disabilities (Monat-Haller, 1992; Sobsey and Mansell, 1990). Knowing about sexuality is essential for recognizing sexual abuse and that, in turn, is essential for controlling risks. Unless children understand something of sexual interactions, they cannot make informed choices about participation (Sobsey, 1994).

Paradoxically, the children who depend on others for daily hygiene are the ones least likely to be given information about their bodies or their rights. In her study of developmentally disabled females, Hard (1986) found an unacceptably high correlation between the lack of sex education and sexual victimization. All of the intellectually disabled girls who were deprived of sex education had been sexually abused, compared with only 12 per cent of those who received sex education. Sobsey (1994) also confirms that the risk of sexual abuse increases with the level of disability.[1]

Children are not asexual. If we fail to provide them with knowledge about their bodies, they acquire inappropriate information from others. Even in relatively closed residential institutions, children are exposed to pornography (Sengstock and Vergason, 1970; Senn, 1988). Uninformed children are also at high risk of abuse by caregivers or older residents (Musick, 1984) or witness the abuse of others (Duffet cited in Senn, 1988, p. 43). Hard (1986) and other researchers found that females with developmental disabilities learned all that they knew about sex from their own abusive experiences. As Senn says, the situation is intolerable.

Researchers have noted that parents, caregivers and teachers often deny the sexuality of children with disabilities and they resist efforts to provide either sex education or child protection programs. Healthy sexual curiosity is repressed, with the result that adolescents have no opportunity to satisfy their sexual urges. This further increases the potential for sexual offences and victimization. When children do not understand what is happening to them, they are unlikely to say, 'No' to inappropriate behaviour (Blomberg, 1986; Forchuk et al., 1984; Goodman, 1973; Hard, 1986; Moglia, 1986; Rose, 1986; Sengstock and Vergason, 1970; Senn, 1988). Kept in ignorance, children are vulnerable to incentives offered by offenders. At greatest risk are those living away from their families with few personal posses-

---

1   For further reading on sex education for children with disabilities see Brown and Craft (1989) and Craft (1987). Many materials are now available for guiding program development but no standard training materials will meet the needs of all students. Programs must be individualized to fit the abilities and situations of students.

sions, freedoms and treats (Senn, 1988; Mitchell, 1985). It is most difficult for children with developmental disabilities to recognize and avoid tricks, bribes and blackmail that abusers use to seduce their victims (PACER, 1986). Sobsey (1994) confirms that the more serious the disability, the higher the risk of sexual abuse.

Disclosures of child sexual abuse are often ignored when made by children with disabilities

International research shows that when children with disabilities report cases of sexual abuse, the reports are less likely to be taken seriously than are those made by non disabled children, and offenders are more likely to be given 'the benefit of the doubt'. Failure to protect disabled children can be attributed to:

- the myths which surround sexual abuse and disability; if we believe that child sexual abuse is committed by strangers and that adults are unlikely to choose sexual partners who do not match our own perceptions of sexual attractiveness, we can ignore cries for help without suffering pangs of conscience;

- society's belief that children and disabled people are (and should remain) asexual. To accept that abuse has occurred, recipients of information have to face aspects of disability and sexuality that they find unpalatable. When we deny children's sexuality, we are likely to convince ourselves that the child misunderstood what happened or, being 'mentally subnormal', that he or she 'made it up'. A recent survey of 80 professionals employed in services for children with disabilities in South Australia showed that none of the health professionals and only two of the teachers would report allegations of sexual abuse made by children with intellectual or severe physical disabilities (Briggs, 1994). Children with developmental disabilities were the ones least likely to be believed. An alarming number of professionals said that they would inform the accused perpetrator (and no one else) of the complaint with the mistaken expectation that, if the allegations were true, the behaviour would stop. What is most alarming about these findings is that all of the professionals involved in the study were mandated to report suspicions of child maltreatment to statutory authorities;

- the physical isolation of teachers and caregivers in special education units ensures that they are often overlooked when in-service programs are offered to teachers in mainstream schools. They are also the ones least likely to have access to resources for teaching personal safety skills and the ones least supported when children have been abused. Disillusionment also inhibits reporting. Conscientious teachers become cynical when statutory authorities fail to investigate allegations, leaving perpetrators free to abuse victims with disabilities;

- adults collude to protect each other when clients complain; this is especially likely when offenders are caregivers and professionals.

Most adults are embarrassed by sexual abuse. Neither professionals nor parents are adequately prepared to receive disclosures. When the reputation of a family, the institution, a colleague or parent is at stake, staff who do not understand the importance of child protection are likely to support the accused with a strong display of group solidarity. Professionals who report their concerns to the management are often persuaded that they misinterpreted what they saw or what they heard and the offender 'wouldn't dream of doing anything like that. He/she loves these kids'. Reporters are regarded as dirty minded trouble makers who made a terrible mistake. Feeling guilty, they withdraw their support for the victim.

Children know that adults collude and that is why they are reluctant to reveal their terrible secrets about sexual abuse (Briggs, 1991a; Briggs and Hawkins, 1994b).

Sexism is involved in the acceptance of reports of sexual abuse

In her study of intellectually disabled girls, Susan Hard (1986) found that the gender of victims determines whether they are ignored or helped when they report sexual abuse. More than half of the girls who disclosed abuse were not believed whereas all reports made by boys were taken seriously. Disclosure stopped the abuse of boys (100 per cent) but ended only a quarter of abuse involving girls. When girls were not believed, the abuse continued in 55 per cent of all cases.

This highlights the importance of educating parents, caregivers and school personnel to protect girls who report abuse. It also suggests that we need to examine our own attitudes about heterosexual and homosexual activity.

- Do we view male–female sex as 'normal' and, therefore, less damaging than homosexual sex?

- Do we view male adult–male child abuse as more perverted and, therefore, more damaging than male adult–female child sexual abuse?

- Do societal taboos on homosexuality lead us to believe that we must protect boys from homosexual abuse but heterosexual abuse doesn't really matter?

- Have we accepted the myth that girls with disabilities are indiscriminately affectionate and that victims 'probably asked for it anyway'?

- Have we adopted the belief that girls 'make it up' but boys are reliable?

There is no evidence to suggest that children with developmental or other disabilities are less reliable in disclosing abuse than other children. To the contrary, Blomberg (cited in Senn, 1988) suggest that, as intellectual developmental disability decreases the capacity to lie, it also increases the capacity to tell the truth about sexual abuse.

Children with disabilities are particularly disadvantaged by communication barriers

Children with speech and hearing impairments are vulnerable to child sexual abuse because they either use different communication systems or have inferior communication skills to the majority of people. Children with cerebral palsy who have poor speech, autistic children and others with communication disorders find it extremely difficult to reject and report sexual offences. They seldom have the means to discuss sensitive issues with adults. They are the ones least likely to receive reliable sex information and they are often unaware of the limits of acceptable adult-child behaviour. Until very recently, there were no symbols to represent and communicate sexual concerns. Even now, these symbols are rarely made available to children.

When teachers and parents provide personal safety and sex education, children with restricted communication facilities are likely to miss and/or misinterpret essential detail. Moore, Weiss and Goodwin (1973), studying 74 deaf children over a five year period, found that when speech alone was used to convey a message, only 34 per cent of the content was understood. When speech and speech reading were used, only 56 per cent of the content was understood. When speech, speech reading and finger spelling were used, the proportion increased to 61 per cent, and when all were used together with sign language, 71 per cent of the content was understood. Deficiencies in language indicate that many vital concepts are likely to be missing: 'secret', 'private', 'trust', 'safe', 'rights' and 'stranger' are just a few of the words used in safety education that are difficult for children to comprehend.

These findings tell us that we must use every available communication method to develop safety skills in children with hearing impairments. It cannot be assumed that clear speech indicates a sound understanding of language; there is often a great discrepancy between the two. Oral ability can actually run counter to the development of safety skills. Margaret Kennedy (1990) cites the work of Susan Phoenix (1987) who found that four year old signing deaf children were 'capable of more independent thought and would ask more "who", "why" and "where" questions than oral deaf children. They investigated their environments in a more powerful way. Kennedy noted the same findings when working with non verbal teenage girls in London. Children's ability to question reduces their vulnerability and facilitates both discussion and the therapeutic process. To develop this skill, children need high levels of self-esteem, confidence and independence which, in turn, require supportive homes and schools.

Phoenix, studying deaf children in Ireland, found that deficiencies in communication caused children to 'accept everything that happened to them without thinking why things happened'. They could not fully explain their daily lives other than by giving basic facts. Children in special residential settings are further disadvantaged if their lives are ordered in such a way that they have no control over what they do. They have to get up at a specified time (even at weekends), undertake a specified routine, eat cornflakes, wear uniforms, and their entire day is organized for them by well-meaning adults. These children soon learn that there are no choices and there is no point in questioning their environment: things are done for them and to them. There is a hierarchy of control but the adults always give the orders and children are always subservient. And as Kennedy (1990) points out, accepting what happens without question is precisely what makes children vulnerable to molestation.

Deaf and non verbal children are seldom given the skills or the opportunities to ask questions about sexual behaviour, ensuring that child molesters are safe from the law when they select these children for victimization. The National Deaf Children's Society (UK) has encountered cases where offenders have learned sign language specifically to gain the trust and compliance of potential victims. Abusers know that, even if victims realize that abuse is wrong, they will experience major difficulties in finding help. Abusers can also be confident that, in the event of offences being reported, children with communication problems are unlikely to be accepted as witnesses in court. Neither judges nor lawyers have shown a willingness to accept evidence from children with cerebral palsy in wheelchairs using electronic communicators or computer keyboards. Until they accept all forms of communication, children with disabilities will remain disadvantaged by the justice system. Until this situation changes, they will continue to be at high risk of victimization.

An additional factor in vulnerability is that members of the hearing impaired and non verbal community use touch as part of their normal, daily communication. As a result, the acceptance of touching behaviours may be different in hearing impaired and non verbal children.

Although a government report confirmed that there were 68,000 hearing impaired children in the United Kingdom (O.P.C.S.), Margaret Kennedy (1989) found that there was no special provision for safety, investigatory and therapeutic services for abused children with hearing impairments. An international search showed that no one had considered or was considering the implications of abuse for children with communication problems.

Deaf and non verbal children have two distinct cultures

For children with communication disabilities, life becomes complicated as they attempt to straddle the different cultures of the disabled and non disabled. The deaf child, for example, has to be both bilingual and bi-cultural, straddling the cultures of the hearing and the deaf. There are different languages to be learned (e.g. sign language and spoken English) as well as different value systems, practices and historical bases. The deaf culture in the English speaking world is noted for its strong conservatism and its acceptance of stereotyped sex roles.

A successful deaf university student told the author, 'The deaf community is dominated by older members who expect us to adopt their values and think and behave like them. They feel safe when they are together and, in some ways, they regard the hearing world as their enemy. I am regarded as a traitor because I see myself as different only in my dependence on technology for hearing. The values of the two communities are very different. And although child abuse has been discussed in the hearing community for the last ten years, no one in the deaf community has permission to mention the subject'.

Few deaf children enjoy equal acceptance in both communities. For the child in the deaf family, deafness is 'normal' and people's reactions are relatively predictable. When deaf children move into the hearing community, however, their deafness may be regarded as a fundamental deficiency.

Deaf children are often immature, insecure, dependent, malleable and lacking in confidence and self-esteem. These characteristics are not the consequence of auditory deprivation itself but the result of children's experience (Schlesinger and Meadow cited in Kennedy, 1973). They are also the characteristics which make deaf and non verbal children highly vulnerable to sexual abuse.

Many people believe that sexual abuse does not harm children with disabilities

One of the factors which enables parents and professionals to 'turn a blind eye' to the abuse of children with disabilities is the myth that abuse is less damaging and less serious when victims are physically or intellectually disabled. The risk of abuse being ignored is especially high when adults believe that victims do not fully understand what happened and that they will quickly forget about it if no one mentions it again. The belief that abuse is less damaging for disabled children also contributes to their selection for abuse by family members.

The reality is that children with disabilities typically suffer the most violent, severe and chronic forms of sexual abuse involving multiple perpetrators (Ammerman et al., 1989; Ryan, 1992; Sobsey, 1994). In up to 67 per cent of cases, anal or vaginal penetration is involved. Research shows that disabled children are just as likely to be damaged by abuse as non disabled children. Sexual abuse results in severe emotional damage which is characterized by internalized anxieties and externalized rage. Studies show that all victims with disabilities lose the capacity to trust other people and they exhibit multiple problems that were not present prior to the abuse (Garbarino *et al.*, 1987). About two thirds of victims show extraordinary fears and, not surprisingly, they experience problems at school. A third experience sleep disturbances and slightly fewer exhibit regressive behaviours. Poor peer relationships are common and some victims resort to self-destructive behaviours.

Of even greater concern is the finding that 37 per cent of victims with disabilities become 'promiscuous', and more than two thirds re-enact the abuse with toys, dolls and other children, perpetuating the abuse cycle and creating another generation of young victims.

Irrespective of the degree of disability, victims feel just as betrayed, stigmatized and powerless as their non disabled counterparts, especially when the offender is a trusted caregiver. This creates problems in all their interpersonal relationships.

Abuse exaggerates children's emotional problems which relate to their disabilities

In her work with deaf victims of sexual abuse, Margaret Kennedy (1990) concluded that abuse compounds the emotional problems associated with disability. Both abuse and disability can produce the following emotional states:

A sense of isolation	Withdrawal
Low self-esteem	Feelings of rejection
Confusion	Depression
Anxiety	Self blame
Powerlessness	Frustration
Anger	Fear
Embarrassment	Stigmatization

Anger relating to the disability focuses on God, the family and peers, particularly on God and the family (for failing to provide protection from the abuser).

Hatred can focus on hearing aids, sticks, wheelchairs, treatment and the disability; the abuse adds an additional dimension: hatred of sexuality and the offender.

Confusion results in questioning, 'Why did this (the disability) happen to me? Why did the abuse happen to me? Why doesn't it happen to others?'

Powerlessness resultioning from disability is duplicated by sexual abuse.

Stigmatization comes from the negative reactions of others to the disability and the disclosure of abuse. Even when the child is believed, few parents or professionals know how to handle and interact with victims supportively in their respective settings. Parents may ignore children's disclosures when they fear that reporting offences will necessitate removing the child from the school or residential situation and there are no alternative services readily available. Mothers may also minimize or reject complaints if they and other members of the family are economically or emotionally dependent upon the abuser. It is easier to believe that a child is lying, at fault or unharmed than tackle the awful reality that a partner is a child molester. Rejection, blame and disbelief increase the victim's feelings of being dirty, used, trapped and valueless.

Although some disabled children may appear to emerge with little emotional disturbance, the data suggest that all are traumatized and require immediate therapeutic intervention (Garbarino *et al.*, p.135).

Summary of the reasons why disabled children are at higher risk of sexual abuse than non disabled children

Children with disabilities are at higher risk of sexual abuse than non disabled children when they are:

- in the care of adults who have accepted the myths relating to the abuse of children with disabilities
- kept ignorant of their rights
- devalued and dehumanized by society
- not adequately protected by child care, education and justice services
- deprived of information about their sexuality, the limits of acceptable adult behaviour and their rights to reject unwanted touching
- dependent on adults for day to day care, becoming compliant and malleable and unlikely to know that they can take control of some aspects of their lives
- deprived of parental affection and approval
- over protected with few opportunities for independence and problem solving
- unable to receive or communicate information about sexual matters
- lacking the confidence and assertiveness needed to complain
- unable to distinguish between acceptable and unacceptable touching due to the quantity of touching involved in their everyday care.

In addition, child victims with disabilities are the ones most likely to:

- have been abused by their caregivers
- suffer violent and prolonged abuse by multiple perpetrators
- be disbelieved or ignored when they report abuse
- be interviewed by professionals who have no specialist skills in communicating with children with special needs when abuse is reported
- to be deprived of justice and therapy, increasing their vulnerability to severe emotional disturbance, re-abuse and re-enactment of the abuse with other children.

Implications for institutions responsible for the care and education of children with disabilities

Because children with disabilities are most likely to be abused by people involved in services relating to their care and education, institutions providing services have four responsibilities:

- the provision of community, parent and staff education to dispel the myths that surround disability, sexuality and sexual abuse
- the provision of support for staff and parents, the majority of whom are caring and concerned people
- the provision of curricula and opportunities for children to learn and practice assertiveness and personal safety skills with the participation of their parents
- the provision of appropriate supervision, especially in residential schools, given that inadequate supervision has been cited as a major factor in the

abuse of children with hearing impairments (Mounty and Fetterman, 1989).

Responsible teachers and care assistants may feel threatened by the research findings presented in this chapter. Some may fear that, when they touch children, their actions could be misinterpreted. Some male child care workers now refuse to cuddle and toilet young children because they are afraid of wrongful accusation. This is a pity because all children need to be hugged and cuddled from time to time and it is especially damaging if adults transfer their own uncomfortable feelings to children in their care.

Barnardos, Newcastle upon Tyne (UK), found that, when foster parents were informed of the high incidence of sexual abuse involving foster families and foster children, the foster parents panicked and demanded complete loyalty from the management of the organization. They sought a *carte blanche* assurance that, in the event of a complaint, they would be believed in preference to their foster children. They also demanded an unconditional guarantee that the service provided would pay for legal aid if they were accused. They sought an assurance of re-employment if they were reported but not convicted of child abuse. When employers were unable to give those assurances, foster parents were angry and afraid.

Professionals often resent having to change their practices even when the reasons for change are explained and make good sense. Staff of institutions which care for children with disabilities should routinely receive new information about child sexual abuse and its effects on victims. After they have had time to absorb this information, they should be encouraged to discuss their anxieties in an open, unemotional forum. In such groups, it may be necessary to give reminders that our own feelings must remain secondary to children's needs and safety.

3 Parent Participation in Personal Safety Programs

Preparing staff for working with children's parents and caregivers in personal safety programs

American, Australian and New Zealand research shows that the most effective child protection programs are those which involve children's primary caregivers. This is especially important when working with young and disabled children (Schroeder, 1994). Unless caregivers participate and accept the need for personal safety skills, they are unlikely to provide the necessary opportunities for children to practise what has been taught in school and they may unwittingly negate that teaching.

Inexperienced teachers are uneasy about involving parents in their child protection programs. Discomfort usually relates to inadequate knowledge and inadequate support. When parents sense a teacher's unease, they, in turn, become apprehensive about the curriculum.

The protection of children with disabilities requires the participation of everyone involved in their care. Ideally, professional development programs should be made available to all school and care-giving personnel (including school bus and taxi drivers, care attendants, health workers, cleaners and voluntary helpers). Separate group sessions are also needed to enlist the cooperation and involvement of children's families.

New Zealand education authorities recognized the need for consistent teaching, strong teacher support and parent involvement when they designed the national curriculum, 'Keeping Ourselves Safe'. Each school has a program coordinator (often the staff member responsible for health education) who has access to a specialist educator employed by New Zealand Police. The coordinator supports individual teachers, makes provision for their professional development, contacts local child protection professionals and arranges school–home communications and parent meetings. New Zealand curriculum designers built parent participation and evaluation into every stage of the program. Parents learn how to reinforce safety concepts at home, how to provide opportunities for practice and how to test children to find out what they have learned. This is clearly the most effective way to go but it involves the commitment of the whole school. If that commitment is lacking, it is better for one teacher to provide quality education for one class (or even the whole school) than to have no provision at all. If a specialist teacher is employed for this purpose, class teachers should always be present during sessions so that safety strategies can be integrated into other aspects of the curriculum.

Most people are influenced by the myths and taboos surrounding both sexual abuse and disability. Anxious teachers fear that the introduction of education for child protection may arouse fears and legitimate concerns in the community. In the early stages, they are unlikely to feel sufficiently confident to respond convincingly to parents' concerns. When there is a school commitment to child protection, coordinators make provision for all staff members to air their anxieties and clarify their attitudes about sexual matters and disability in a non threatening environment, preferably with the help of someone who has expertise in child protection and counselling skills.

Male staff members are often the ones who feel most threatened by the introduction of child protection programs. This is because of the publicity given to the fact that most sex offences are committed by men. Uncomfortable men need to be reminded that more than a third of abused boys are also victimized by females and all abuse is damaging, regardless of the gender of the perpetrator.

Men who were not victimized in childhood find it hard to understand why anyone would want to use children for sexual satisfaction. They are bewildered and shocked by rape and embarrassed by their own maleness. Uncomfortable people avoid the literature and television documentaries about child abuse. As a result, their views are often based on myths, fears and rumours. They tend to deny the size or importance of the problem and worry that, if children are informed and empowered, they will misuse that power to make malicious allegations. All of these and other anxieties should be discussed thoroughly and non judgementally.

Professional support is very important for teachers because, when they lack confidence, they are likely to select the non-controversial parts of a program, omitting the sensitive and most important sessions to reduce the risk of having to deal with a disclosure.

Sixty-four per cent of teachers who claimed to be using 'Protective Behaviours' in South Australian schools omitted the only sessions which would have told children about their rights if they became the targets for sexual misbehaviour (Briggs, 1991a). The excuses given for these omissions were:

- 'There wasn't enough time.'
- 'The parents wouldn't want it.'
- 'These children aren't ready for it.'
- 'It isn't necessary: child abuse isn't a problem at this school.'
- 'I didn't feel sufficiently confident to handle this part of the curriculum.'

None of these excuses is valid. When a personal safety program is introduced, parents have the right to expect the school to provide all the information that children need to stay safe from sexual abuse.

'Parents in this neighbourhood won't want their children to be taught personal safety skills' is the reason commonly given by teachers to defend their neglect of safety issues in the school curriculum. Usually this means that parents have not been invited to express an opinion. In a random survey of parents responsible for 568 Australian families, all said that they wanted schools to teach personal safety skills because they lacked the knowledge and confidence to undertake the task themselves (Briggs, 1987). These findings confirm those of Finkelhor in Boston, Mass., (1984).

How can we interest parents in their children's protection?

Although school-based child protection programs have been well received by parents in Canada, the United States, Australia and New Zealand, most parents underestimate the risks for their own children. The literature shows that only 22 per cent of Australian parents and a third of New Zealand and American parents accepted invitations to attend school information meetings to introduce child protection curriculum (Briggs, 1991; Mayes *et al.*, 1992). Australian parents gave the following reasons for their non attendance:

- I trust the school's choice of program and am happy to leave it entirely in the teachers' hands.

- Child protection is an unpleasant subject and I'd rather not know about it.

- Ours isn't that kind of family.

- I trust all our friends and neighbours (etc.) and our children are not at risk.

- The timing of the meeting was inappropriate.

This suggests that we have to devise strategies to convince parents of their importance in their children's protection.

Another recent finding is that when parent participation is limited to a single information session, that session has little or no impact on parents' complacent attitudes (Berrick, 1988). Most parents attend the first meeting to gain confirmation that their family is immune from the abuse problem and that there is no need for them to become involved. They 'switch off' in the face of a bombardment of uncomfortable information and retain the myths. For maximum effectiveness, the introductory meeting should be followed by regular workshops at which parents have the opportunity to rethink their ideas and work out how they can make the best contribution to their children's education.

School–home communications must be carefully planned

When a child protection program is planned, a letter should be sent to all parents inviting them to attend the information session (see sample letter). Communications should stress the fact that, in safety matters, parents are children's most important teachers and the support of both mothers and fathers is essential. Letters should include the expectation that parents who cannot attend the meeting will suggest appointment times to meet the coordinator or class teacher to discuss how they can help their children.

In multi-cultural communities, teachers should enlist the help of community representatives to send communications in the appropriate community languages.

Fathers are usually hard to convince that they have any contribution to make to children's safety. They regard child protection as 'mother's business' (Briggs, 1988). Unless a child care facility is provided, dads remain at home to 'look after the children'. In ignorance, they are then likely to dismiss their wives' and children's legitimate concerns when aspects of safety are involved.

lacking, it is better for one teacher to provide quality education for one class (or even the whole school) than to have no provision at all. If a specialist teacher is employed for this purpose, class teachers should always be present during sessions so that safety strategies can be integrated into other aspects of the curriculum.

Most people are influenced by the myths and taboos surrounding both sexual abuse and disability. Anxious teachers fear that the introduction of education for child protection may arouse fears and legitimate concerns in the community. In the early stages, they are unlikely to feel sufficiently confident to respond convincingly to parents' concerns. When there is a school commitment to child protection, coordinators make provision for all staff members to air their anxieties and clarify their attitudes about sexual matters and disability in a non threatening environment, preferably with the help of someone who has expertise in child protection and counselling skills.

Male staff members are often the ones who feel most threatened by the introduction of child protection programs. This is because of the publicity given to the fact that most sex offences are committed by men. Uncomfortable men need to be reminded that more than a third of abused boys are also victimized by females and all abuse is damaging, regardless of the gender of the perpetrator.

Men who were not victimized in childhood find it hard to understand why anyone would want to use children for sexual satisfaction. They are bewildered and shocked by rape and embarrassed by their own maleness. Uncomfortable people avoid the literature and television documentaries about child abuse. As a result, their views are often based on myths, fears and rumours. They tend to deny the size or importance of the problem and worry that, if children are informed and empowered, they will misuse that power to make malicious allegations. All of these and other anxieties should be discussed thoroughly and non judgementally.

Professional support is very important for teachers because, when they lack confidence, they are likely to select the non-controversial parts of a program, omitting the sensitive and most important sessions to reduce the risk of having to deal with a disclosure.

Sixty-four per cent of teachers who claimed to be using 'Protective Behaviours' in South Australian schools omitted the only sessions which would have told children about their rights if they became the targets for sexual misbehaviour (Briggs, 1991a). The excuses given for these omissions were:

- 'There wasn't enough time.'
- 'The parents wouldn't want it.'
- 'These children aren't ready for it.'
- 'It isn't necessary: child abuse isn't a problem at this school.'
- 'I didn't feel sufficiently confident to handle this part of the curriculum.'

None of these excuses is valid. When a personal safety program is introduced, parents have the right to expect the school to provide all the information that children need to stay safe from sexual abuse.

'Parents in this neighbourhood won't want their children to be taught personal safety skills' is the reason commonly given by teachers to defend their neglect of safety issues in the school curriculum. Usually this means that parents have not been invited to express an opinion. In a random survey of parents responsible for 568 Australian families, all said that they wanted schools to teach personal safety skills because they lacked the knowledge and confidence to undertake the task

Sample of return slip for notification of attendance at parents' training workshops

Please tick which sentence is appropriate and return this slip to your child's teacher by .... 199.. .

❑ We will attend the workshops together.

❑ I will attend the workshop alone.

❑ I will require the use of the child care facility for my children aged ....

I am unable to attend the workshops but would like an appointment to discuss the program with you at school on the following date .... (Please give a choice of times).

Monday at:	am/pm	Thursday	am/pm
Tuesday		Friday	
Wednesday			

From ....

Address

....

....

Telephone number ....

This return slip is often effective in attracting the attention of parents who do not normally participate in school affairs. Given that these sessions are unlikely to involve large groups of parents, it will be advisable to make personal contact with those who cannot read the English language and those who fail to reply. If it is known that a child has already been abused, a personal approach should be used.

Ideas for letters from schools to parents:

Dear ....

We are pleased that so many parents attended the 'Safety Skills' evening. Thank you for coming and sharing your ideas with us. Thank you for listening to our ideas, too.

We realize that some parents will not be able to attend all of the meetings and hope that you will ask questions and let us know of your child's progress. This week, we are talking about our bodies. We are trying to teach children that they have a responsibility to keep their bodies safe and well. In the next few days, we shall check that children know the correct names for all parts of their bodies. They will learn that some parts of their bodies are private.

We are also making efforts to improve children's self-confidence. Children's safety depends on their ability to assert themselves at the right time. This depends on them feeling good about themselves. They also need practice.

I am enclosing some of the work that _____ has completed this week.

We thank you for your support.

If you have any queries, please jot them down, call in or telephone us.

Yours sincerely

(Senior teacher and class teacher)

Dear ....

Thank you for your interest in and support for our child protection program. This week, we are helping children to become more aware of their feelings so that when they feel worried, scared or unsafe, they will do something to make themselves feel safer. Today, we asked children to think about the different kinds of feelings that people have. We will try to teach them to tune in to their feelings so that they recognize when they are not safe.

This week's homework: please talk to _____ about the worksheets that he/she has done at school and share some of your own scary feelings.

Yours sincerely

(Senior teacher and class teacher)

Dear ....

This week we spent more time talking about what we can do if we get scary feelings. We practised taking action in pretend situations in which we might find ourselves and need help. We invited children to think about which trustworthy people they could turn to for help. Unfortunately, busy adults don't always listen to children when they are worried about something. So, we have to teach children to persist in getting help until someone DOES something or something happens to make them feel safe again. It is not sufficient to say 'Tell someone' because, even when adults hear children, they often do nothing to make them safer.

This week's homework : As part of our protection program, we would like all children to know their names, addresses, telephone numbers and the contact numbers of parents when they are at work.

Yours sincerely

(Senior teacher and class teacher)

Strategies for maximizing parent participation in programs

If there is a poor response to invitations to attend meetings and workshops, staff should investigate the barriers to participation and devise strategies to overcome them; for example, parents are less likely to attend if they

- underestimate their own importance in child protection
- lack information about the risks to their own children
- lack child care facilities
- have transport problems
- feel uncomfortable in the school environment
- were abused in childhood, and have not dealt with their own emotions and residual fears
- feel powerless and live in unsafe homes.

SCHOOLS MAY FIND SOME OF THE FOLLOWING SUGGESTIONS HELPFUL

- Establish a group of parents, teachers and community members who will develop and implement strategies to increase parent interest and involvement.
- Avoid the use of jargon when sending communications to parents.
- Provide a child care facility with the help of other staff, parents and students.
- Invite interested parents and community members to participate in staff development sessions.
- Seek advice from multi-cultural educational services and community representatives on different cultural mores and expectations.
- Introduce a 'buddy scheme' where supportive parents visit and encourage the participation of the reluctant ones.
- Establish and utilize parents who are willing to provide transport for others.
- Take account of local customs and don't plan meetings for times that clash with popular social activities or late night shopping.
- Consider holding meetings at a more comfortable venue such as the community centre.
- Recruit expert helpers to communicate with deaf parents and those who have a limited knowledge of English.
- Use community languages for posters and publicity.
- Make personal contact with parents of new students and parents who visit the school only rarely.
- Use only ethnic media and community services to publicize school efforts in child protection.
- Ensure that children's work is displayed in rooms used for parent meetings.
- In addition, multi-cultural schools might arrange separate meetings or sub-groups for different language groups and involve bilingual speakers.

BEFORE THE MEETING:

- Select a chair person.

- Have curriculum materials readily available.

- Send a press release to gain the support of local media.

- Arrange for visiting speakers, videos and equipment.

- Ensure that responsible people are in charge of child care arrangements and refreshments.

- Ensure that enough copies of documents have been printed for distribution.

- Invite and introduce community members whose work focuses on child protection.

- Invite a bookseller who specializes in the sale of books for personal growth to display appropriate literature.

THE AIMS OF THE PROGRAM ARE TO HELP CHILDREN TO IDENTIFY AND AVOID POTENTIALLY DANGEROUS SITUATIONS AND:

- improve their decision making and problem solving skills

- improve their communication skills and openness with parents

- help to develop their capacity for independence with safety

- develop their confidence and self-esteem

- encourage equality in relationships.

THE OBJECTIVES OF PARENT PARTICIPATION IN THE PROGRAM MAY BE TO:

- develop knowledge about the nature and extent of child sexual abuse

- become familiar with the aims of the school program

- reinforce concepts and skills in the home

- become sufficiently confident and knowledgeable to talk to children about sexual misbehaviour so that children can disclose concerns

- respond to children's disclosures about sexual misbehaviour supportively and effectively

- help parents to change parenting styles which might increase children's vulnerability to abuse

- provide opportunities for communications with school staff and local child protection personnel.

Some suggestions for topics for the first parents' meeting

○ Welcome and introduction of staff and community representatives.

○ What is sexual abuse?

Define sexual abuse as when an older, bigger, more powerful or more knowledgeable child, adolescent or adult uses a weaker or less well informed child for sexual gratification. This then includes the abuse of an intellectually disabled child by others of a similar age who, by virtue of being better informed, are more powerful.

○ The size of the problem.

○ Why do you think that children are vulnerable to sexual abuse?

○ Why are children with disabilities at greatest risk of sexual abuse?

○ Who are the offenders?

Dispense with the myth of the dangerous stranger: children with disabilities are at greatest risk from people involved in their care. Abusers go to a great deal of trouble to develop the trust of parents and school staff so that when children complain about what is happening, they are disbelieved.

The only characteristic that offenders have in common is that most were badly damaged by sexual abuse in childhood. Many began offending at puberty or earlier and nothing has happened to stop them.

Ask the questions: 'Why is it that child molesters manage to molest hundreds of children without being caught?'

'Where are sexual offences most likely to occur?'

Bear in mind that offenders can be male or female.

○ Who are the victims?

Dispense with the myth that it only happens to older children and that girls are at much greater risk of sexual abuse than boys. Recent research shows that the abuse of boys is seldom reported, not because it doesn't happen but, on the contrary, because it is so widespread that victims regard it as 'normal'. Boys are more likely than girls to be abused in groups and they rarely complain if abuse was non violent and they did not resist.

○ Why children don't tell their parents when someone behaves sexually.

Ask the question: Could you have told your parents about sexual misbehaviour? If not, why not? Who could you have told?

If children tell anyone at all, they tell a trusted friend to keep a secret. Why?

Please ensure that children's fears are discussed including:

• boys' fears relating to the taboo surrounding homosexuality

• the fear of punishment because the abuse happened

• being disbelieved by parents

• fear of the abuser and the threats used to maintain secrecy: e.g. that police will take them away and put them into a home for bad kids

• fear of family break up.

In addition, children keep abuse secret because of:

• embarrassment

• self blame

• guilt

• shame

• dependence on the offender

• adults' taboos on communications relating to sexual matters

• ignorance – the child grew up with abuse and thinks it is normal

- child molesters invariably convince children that they caused the abuse.

○ Why do you think it is important to stop child sexual abuse?

Contrary to the expectations of many parents, child victims do not forget abuse. Apart from the damage to their sexual and psychological development, their health and their capacity to create trusting relationships, it is estimated that a quarter of male victims become offenders.

○ Given that most child victims know their abusers, what kind of information and skills do children need to protect themselves from the risk of abuse?

Point out that, although this subject is distressing, the reality of abuse is very much worse. Because of recent knowledge, we can do a great deal more now than we have done in the past to prevent it from happening and help children to stay safe.

○ Why is parent support crucial?

Parents can unwittingly undermine child protection education, for example by

- teaching children that they must never say 'No' to adults
- indicating that children must tolerate unwanted touching to please adult relatives
- depriving children of opportunities for independence
- depriving children of knowledge about their sexuality
- teaching children to keep family secrets
- punishing children for attempting to practice assertiveness
- telling children to 'be good and do as XXX (the babysitter) says', equating goodness with complete obedience
- using 'pet' names for genitals that no one else understands
- creating a taboo on sexuality so that there is no scope for communication
- discouraging boys from expressing feelings and seeking physical affection.

Physical affection between fathers and sons is especially important for the protection of boys. Children with disabilities are at especially high risk if they feel that they are not valued at home.

○ About the program.

Present a sample of the first lesson and ask parents how they think that they can help children to practise problem solving and skill development outside the classroom.

○ Questions.

○ Plans for future workshops.

○ Refreshments.

Handling parents' concerns about child protection programs

The concerns that parents commonly express relate to:

- the relevance and appropriateness of the program to their children's level of development
- possible effects on their children
- possible effects on home life
- the possibility that the program will teach their children to challenge adult authority
- the appropriateness of teaching children to use the correct anatomical names for genitals
- teacher expertise
- the provision of opportunities for ongoing consultation with teachers
- how the family can help.

Parents should be assured that sessions will be planned to meet the different needs and abilities of each child. Some children will grasp a concept quite quickly; others will need lots of practice and repetition before anything is learned thoroughly. Parents can be closely involved in the repetition through carefully planned 'homework'.

When parents adopt negative attitudes to child protection programs, their views are usually based on the myths relating to child sexual abuse, disability and safety education. There are almost as many myths surrounding protective education as surround child abuse itself. Some are promoted by offenders who have a vested interest in keeping children ignorant. Some are promoted by well-intentioned but misguided conservatives who believe that we can maintain children's 'innocence' and keep them asexual by depriving them of knowledge about their bodies. Most are the result of a community refusal to accept the seriousness of the child abuse problem. It is best to tackle concerns at the very beginning; there is sufficient information in Parts One and Two of this book to respond to anxieties relating to the relevance of child protection programs to children with disabilities. Other common questions (and answers) are listed below.

Parents' fears relating to the possible effects on children

QUESTION: 'MIGHT THE PROGRAM ALARM CHILDREN UNNECESSARILY AND MAKE THEM DISTRUST ALL ADULTS?'

It should be pointed out that a road safety program does not make children afraid of travelling and a lesson on water safety does not make children afraid of swimming. By the same token, developmentally appropriate personal safety education should not make children afraid of people; to the contrary, when children understand their rights and are assured of parental support, their confidence increases. Surveys of parents in South Australia and the USA (Finkelhor and Strapko, 1987) showed that parents found their children to be more open and less fearful after involvement in personal safety programs. Staying safe with others is just one of many skills that children need for survival. Children also need to know how to stay safe with fire, electricity, drugs and other poisonous substances.

QUESTION: 'WILL A PERSONAL SAFETY PROGRAM PLACE AN UNFAIR RESPONSIBILITY ON CHILDREN FOR KEEPING THEMSELVES SAFE WITH ADULTS?'

No, on the contrary, we, the adults, place unfair responsibilities on children when we send them out into the world lacking knowledge of the acceptable limits of adult behaviour.

QUESTION: 'AREN'T THESE CHILDREN TOO YOUNG TO KNOW THE CORRECT ANATOMICAL NAMES FOR GENITALS?'

As shown on page 6 of this book, there is an irrational avoidance of the use of anatomically correct names for body parts in the genital area. This relates to the long standing taboo surrounding sexuality itself. Parents realize the absurdity of their concerns when teachers explain the negative consequences of failing to give children the adult vocabulary for all parts of the body.

QUESTION: 'WON'T PERSONAL SAFETY EDUCATION TEACH CHILDREN ABOUT SEX LONG BEFORE THEY ARE OLD ENOUGH TO UNDERSTAND?'

First, children are sexual beings who learn about sex from experimentation, their peers, abuse and the media. Without developmentally appropriate sex education, their knowledge is often faulty. Faulty knowledge can be dangerous and it may result in unnecessary fears. Child molesters often seduce uninformed children by pretending to teach them about sex.

Second, personal safety programs are about safety, not sex. However, it is strongly recommended that children with disabilities are taught about their bodies because of the very high correlation between sexual ignorance and victimization, especially the victimization of children with developmental disabilities. This is the task of a specialist sex educator, not the class teacher.

QUESTION: 'TO KEEP CHILDREN SAFE, DON'T YOU HAVE TO TEACH THEM ABOUT DEVIANT SEX?'

It is important that children are given clear guidelines about handling the most common forms of sexual misbehaviour because, without that information, children are likely to remain confused about what they are supposed to avoid and report. Confusion causes more anxiety than the information itself.

It also needs to be emphasized that, if adults avoid important facts, child victims realize that what happened to them is so disgusting that it cannot be mentioned. Furthermore, as indicated on pages 17 and 21 of this book, without specific information about acceptable and unacceptable behaviour, children with disabilities are very likely to learn about sex by being abused.

Parents need to be assured that sessions are taught in a positive classroom environment which aims to build the participants' self-esteem and their ability to identify and deal with threatening situations. To allay parents' fears about the program, teachers should inform them about the overall content and how they can help.

Parents who worry about talking to children about sexual matters should be referred to the booklets available on this topic.

QUESTION: 'WILL THE PROGRAM MAKE CHILDREN DISTRUST THEIR PARENTS?'

One of the myths promoted by opponents of education for child protection was that personal safety programs are designed by militant feminists to destroy the family unit and make children distrust their fathers.

The pioneers of protective education were certainly supported by the feminist movement but the major programs now used in schools are the work of multi-professional teams. The Canadian CARE Kit was inspired by the Royal Canadian

Mounted Police with a team of parents and professionals and it was evaluated by academics at the University of British Columbia. New Zealand's 'Keeping Ourselves Safe' was a joint Police and Education Department effort, taking six years to complete the primary school curriculum. Evaluation and revision is a continuous process. This book is also the result of teamwork by a group of professionals whose credentials are provided in the preface.

QUESTION: 'WHEN CHILDREN LEARN ABOUT THEIR RIGHTS, WON'T THEY MAKE UP STORIES ABOUT ABUSE TO "GET EVEN" WITH PEOPLE WHO DISCIPLINE THEM?'

An international search produced no research evidence to support the suggestion that children fabricate allegations of sexual abuse: on the contrary, sexual abuse is so embarrassing that children understate what actually happened to them. When children retract allegations of sexual abuse and say, 'I made it up', it is usually because they are being subjected to pressures or threats from the offender and relatives.

QUESTION: 'IS THERE A RISK THAT THE PROGRAM WILL INTERFERE WITH THE FREE EXPRESSION OF PHYSICAL AFFECTION, FOR EXAMPLE, BETWEEN FATHERS AND DAUGHTERS?'

Parents often feel threatened when they learn that children will be taught about their rights. A common fear is that, 'If I pat my child's bottom playfully and she tells the teacher, I might be reported and charged with child sexual abuse'.

Parents should be assured that no social worker or police officer could take legal action without substantive evidence that an offence has occurred.

Confusion about father–child relationships and expressions of affection is most likely when unacceptable behaviour is not clearly defined.

Parents need to know that family relationships improve when children realize that their parents will help them to stop unwanted behaviour (Briggs, 1991a, 1991b; Wurtele, 1993). Furthermore, Plummer (1986) found that, after participating in education about child sexual assault, children become more positive about genuine expressions of affection.

QUESTION: 'WILL THE PROGRAM TEACH CHILDREN TO CHALLENGE ADULT AUTHORITY?'

One of the most common fears expressed by both parents and teachers is that children will be taught to challenge adult authority and that they will become disobedient and say 'No' to legitimate requests.

Parents need to know that personal safety programs tell children that they can say 'No' to sexual misbehaviour, unsafe situations and touching which makes them feel uncomfortable. Without that teaching, children believe that they have to tolerate everything that adults do to them. This makes them highly vulnerable to sexual abuse (Briggs, 1991).

Of course children make mistakes when practising new skills. Some parents complain that their offspring refuse to go to bed or refuse to have a bath after a session on learning to say 'No'. These problems are easily resolved with reminders that children *can* say 'No' when asked to do something that is wrong or unsafe. This affirmation should be followed by a brief enquiry as to why it is wrong or unsafe to take a bath or go to bed.

When parents and teachers cooperate in providing opportunities for problem solving and decision making, children soon learn to differentiate between situations in which they can and should assert their rights as distinct from safe situations that they dislike and would like to avoid, such as going to bed at the right time, having a bath or helping with jobs in the house.

While the program encourages the growth of independence, the continuing major role of parents must be acknowledged.

QUESTION: 'ISN'T THE PROBLEM OF CHILD SEXUAL ABUSE EXAGGERATED? SHOULD WE EXPOSE ALL CHILDREN TO PERSONAL SAFETY EDUCATION JUST BECAUSE A FEW ARE AT RISK?'

International conferences and governments confirm that child sexual abuse is a worldwide concern and the number of offences reported represents only the fringe of the problem. Of 190 male sexual abuse victims interviewed by the author (Briggs and Hawkins 1994a), only 14 per cent disclosed abuse and the disclosures were made in adolescence after several years of suffering. All of the victims were multiply abused by multiple perpetrators over several years. Only two offenders were reported to police. In other words, report statistics, in this case, represented less than 1 per cent of the problem.

Uncomfortable adults

The people most likely to cling to myths about personal safety programs are those who have not come to terms with their own sexuality. They find it difficult to talk about the human body. They avoid any acknowledgement of the sexual development of disabled children and hope to keep them asexual by isolating them in ignorance.

By the law of averages, in any group of parents, teachers or caregivers, there will be some survivors of child sexual abuse. If they have not confronted their emotions, the discussion of personal safety is likely to bring back unwanted reminders. If survivors still have strong angry or guilty feelings about what happened, they will find it difficult to provide protection for children who need help. When these adult survivors come to notice, they should be encouraged to seek counselling from someone who has proven expertise in this field of work. Counsellors can usually be located through Community Health and Rape Crisis Centres.

Workshops for parents

The first information session should be followed by small group workshops to help parents to provide better protection for their children.

Workshops should combine small group discussion and suitable videos to 'get the message home' in a non threatening way. Workshop leaders should assess the needs of individuals in the group and adapt material and teaching styles accordingly. It is helpful if counsellors can also be present.

The following are suggestions for the content of parent workshops.

Introduction

Provide light refreshments before the sessions start to enable participants to relax and get to know each other. In the early stages, use other 'ice-breakers' to help parents to feel comfortable. One possibility is to divide the group into pairs and ask parents to talk about themselves for three minutes. At the end of that time, participants change roles and repeat the process. Each participant then introduces their partner to the whole group.

Discuss society's attitudes to sexuality and people with disabilities

This should provide the opportunity to deal with the myths that surround both sexuality and disability. Group leaders should bear in mind that some parents may not have discussed sexual issues before and there may be some discomfort in the early stages.

In matters of opinion, it is sometimes useful to ask participants to use their bodies to indicate where they stand on certain issues. The leader draws a line across the room to create the notion of a continuum with extreme views at each end.

At this session, it may be useful to involve a disabled person who is knowledgeable about the sexual needs and rights of disabled people.

Find out what parents know about child sexual abuse

Parents will be encouraged to define how they perceive sexual abuse and why disabled children are so vulnerable. It is important to let participants talk so that leaders can listen and understand 'where parents are at' and plan more appropriately for future sessions. A sample questionnaire is provided to encourage parents to say whether the common myths that surround sexual abuse and disabled children are true or false. Each point should be discussed within small groups.

Facts or myths?

Suggestions for a questionnaire to use in workshops. Answers are provided for the benefit of workshop leaders.

STATEMENT: CHILDREN MAKE UP STORIES ABOUT CHILD SEXUAL ABUSE: **TRUE OR FALSE?**

This is false. Children cannot imagine sexual behaviour. Imagination develops from experience. Furthermore, children expect to be punished for disclosing it. They rarely tell anyone about the most horrendous aspects of what happened because they are too distressed. When a child retracts a statement and says, 'I made it up', it is usually because the family is disintegrating and there is no support. The offender's supporters give the victim the impression that, if he or she retracts the statement, all will be well. Usually all is not well: the victim is branded as a liar, sympathy goes to the offender and, confident that no one believes the child, the abuse continues.

STATEMENT: TEENAGE GIRLS SEDUCE THEIR FATHERS: **TRUE OR FALSE?**

This is false. Goldman and Goldman (1988) showed that children do not see their parents as sexual beings. On the contrary, they are embarrassed when parents reveal their sexuality. Sex is viewed in romantic terms and seen as exclusively for the young.

STATEMENT: SEXUAL OFFENCES ARE COMMITTED IN A MOMENT OF WEAKNESS AND ARE USUALLY 'ONE OFF' EVENTS. OFFENDERS ARE NOT LIKELY TO DO IT AGAIN ONCE IT HAS BEEN DISCLOSED. **TRUE OR FALSE?**

Both statements are false. Child molesters are likely to have committed offences against large numbers of children before they are caught. They are also likely to continue offending unless they are apprehended by police, join a sex offenders program and genuinely want to change. If adults ignore incidents of abuse, offenders tend to become more daring because they 'got away with it'.

STATEMENT: IF A CHILD IS ABUSED, IT'S BEST TO FORGET ABOUT IT AND NOT MENTION IT AGAIN. **TRUE OR FALSE?**

False! Victims of sexual offences need expert professional help to work through their strong emotions about the offences and the offender and develop skills in assertiveness to reduce the risk of re-abuse. If victims are not given the opportunity to work through their feelings about the abuse, the feelings may build up and cause greater harm in adolescence or adulthood.

STATEMENT: IT DOESN'T MATTER IF CHILDREN WITH DISABILITIES ARE SEXUALLY ABUSED BECAUSE THEY DON'T HAVE FEELINGS LIKE THE REST OF US. **TRUE OR FALSE?**

False! Sexual abuse is damaging to all children. Victims suffer emotional damage from the abuse of power and trust. Feelings of being used, dirty and inferior are the same whether children have disabilities or not. Victims with developmental disabilities are at high risk of repeating the abuse behaviour, creating a cycle of abuse.

STATEMENT: WHEN PEOPLE ARE RAPED, IT'S USUALLY BECAUSE THEY DID SOMETHING TO DESERVE IT. **TRUE OR FALSE?**

This is a dangerous myth created to transfer blame from rapists to their victims. It is also untrue. Research shows that 60 to 70 per cent of rapists first decide to rape someone then set out to find their victims. Both boys and girls are vulnerable to rape (Garbarino *et al.*, 1987).

STATEMENT: FEMALES DON'T COMMIT SEXUAL OFFENCES. **TRUE OR FALSE?**

False. Women have taken an active part in some of the most horrendous sex crimes in history but sexual offences by women are reported less frequently than offences by men. Sometimes women are lone offenders, whilst some are under the domination of males. In common with male offenders, adolescent and adult females are likely to have been victims of sexual and/or emotional abuse in childhood.

STATEMENT: WE DON'T NEED TO WORRY ABOUT PROTECTING BOYS. **TRUE OR FALSE?**

False. Boys are at high risk of sexual abuse. When they are young, they are abused by older cousins, siblings and other family members. As boys grow older, they are granted more freedom and their social circle widens, increasing the risks of abuse by older peers, neighbours and leaders of social groups for boys.

Boys are at a disadvatage if they do not identify abuse as wrong. When they realize that it should not have happened, they feel ashamed and guilty and are deterred from reporting it by the stigma associated with homosexuality.

The abuse of boys by women is difficult to report because of male cultural attitudes that regard sex with older women as beneficial.

STATEMENT: YOU CAN'T DO ANYTHING TO PROTECT CHILDREN. WHEN THEY ARE OUT OF YOUR SIGHT, YOU JUST HAVE TO PRAY. **TRUE OR FALSE?**

False. Pray if you wish but personal safety skills should be introduced to children when they are about three years old using books such as 'My Body' published by Parenting Press. This introduces the concept that children are responsible for their bodies and have private parts (which should be named). A very good reason for teaching safety skills is that abusers avoid confident children who have been involved in protective programs and are aware of their rights.

STATEMENT: NOBODY WOULD WANT TO MOLEST PHYSICALLY DISABLED CHILDREN IN WHEELCHAIRS. THEY AREN'T ATTRACTIVE. **TRUE OR FALSE?**

False! Apart from the fact that physically disabled people can be sexually attractive to others, sexual offences are not about sexual attractiveness; they are about the abuse of power and the control of the weak by the strong. Sexual abuse is used as a way of denigrating and hurting victims as well as a means of satisfying cravings for sexual activity. Disabled children are selected for the same reasons that lead to the rape of frail old ladies. Their attractiveness lies in their inability to fight back.

STATEMENT: SEXUAL ABUSE DOESN'T HAPPEN IN MIDDLE CLASS COMMUNITIES. **TRUE OF FALSE?**

Sexual abusers come from all walks of life. They are politicians, judges, social workers, teachers and priests. They are scout and camp leaders. No one can be trusted on the basis of their education, social position or even their relationship to a child.

If we tried to teach children to fear all human beings, they would lead very unhappy lives. What we can do is teach them to recognize potentially dangerous situations and take action to make themselves safer.

Attitudes and misconceptions commonly expressed by the non-disabled about people with disabilities

It may be useful to invite group members to list and discuss some of the attitudes commonly expressed by those who have no disabled family members.

The following are some examples:

- Most disabled people would be better off in sheltered workshops.

- Disabled children should be in special schools where they can get plenty of attention.

- People with obvious disabilities make the non disabled feel uncomfortable and they should be kept out of sight.

- People with intellectual disabilities should be locked up somewhere so that they do no harm.

- We should feel sorry for all disabled people.

- Disabled people should be sterilized.

- Disabled kids shouldn't be given sex education: they might experiment.

HELP PARENTS TO IMPROVE COMMUNICATIONS WITH THEIR CHILDREN

When parents are asked 'How would you know if your child had been sexually abused?' they usually reply, 'My child would tell me if something was wrong' or, 'I'd just know by the look in their eyes' (Berrick, 1988).

These statements provide opportunities for helping parents to examine what they have actually done to encourage their children's confidences.

- Have they already talked to their children about sexual matters? What (exactly) was said? How might a child interpret that?

- How do their children know that if they talk about sexual misbehaviour, they will be believed and not punished?

- Have they given their children the vocabulary needed to communicate about sexually related matters?

45

Encourage parents to explore the problems that their children might experience in trying to talk to them about sexual concerns.

Parents need to know that their children will not confide in them unless they have *already demonstrated* that they will listen to their concerns and have shown that they will support them and not blame them (i.e. merely telling them that they can talk about their worries is not enough if it conflicts with children's experiences). There are several useful, short videos available to educate parents on the need to listen to children.

Most children believe that their parents will fuss, be angry, blame, punish them and support the abuser. All too frequently, they are right.

This is a good time to get parents thinking and talking about their own attitudes to sexual matters and how they can provide more realistic protection.

DISCUSS THE DANGERS OF FAMILY SECRECY

Could parents adopt a 'No secrets' policy? Are they aware of the role of secrecy involved in child sexual abuse? How do their children know which secrets to keep and which to tell? Have they ever been reprimanded for disclosing parents' secrets?

HELP PARENTS TO UNDERSTAND THE DYNAMICS OF SEXUAL ABUSE

- How do offenders trick and gain power over children?
- How do they manage to evade the law?
- How seriously should we take offences committed by other children?
- How might a child feel if a trusted adult introduced sexual touching?
- How can children be supported and protected?
- Is an offender likely to stop abusing children if no one reports it? Why?

TEACH PARENTS HOW TO HANDLE SUSPICIONS AND DISCLOSURES OF ABUSE

It is useful if schools invite a trusted, competent and empathic child protection worker or police officer to the session to explain what happens when a case is reported.

START A PARENT LIBRARY OFFERING BOOKS ON CHILD PROTECTION FOR ADULTS AND CHILDREN

The National Committee for Prevention of Child Abuse and ETR Network Publications (USA) have a large variety of useful booklets available. Bookshops catering for human services are sometimes prepared to send displays of relevant books on a 'sale or return' basis. Most social welfare services provide free literature on child protection.

INTRODUCE THE SAFETY CONCEPTS USED IN THE PROGRAM

Parents and teachers should work together on how the basic safety concepts can be practised outside school on a week by week basis. Those who do not attend workshops should be contacted and told how they can help.

Unfortunately, the poorest response is usually that of the parent of the child in the least safe home. A mother may regard personal safety for children as unachievable and a waste of time if she has no control over her own life and lives in fear of domestic violence. Whenever possible, reluctant participants should be contacted directly either by phone or a home visit.

DISCUSS THE REALITY OF THE DANGEROUS STRANGER

Most parents tell children to avoid being kidnapped by dangerous strangers in cars. Because of the complexity of the stranger concept discussed in Part One of this book, this is unrealistic and provides scope for vivid imaginations, resulting in fearfulness, nightmares and inhibitions which can restrict children's lives (Briggs, 1991; Briggs and Hawkins, 1993a, 1993b). Parents will realize how vulnerable their young and developmentally disabled children are if they ask what they know about strangers, have they ever seen a stranger and how they can tell that someone is a stranger?

To stay safe from sexual abuse, children need to be able to identify potentially dangerous situations rather than dangerous people. This skill necessitates providing opportunities for problem solving at home and on outings. When children get lost in a crowded place, they often have to depend on strangers for help. The question that they must resolve for themselves is, which stranger is likely to be the safest person to approach in different circumstances. Who would be the best person to help a child who caught the wrong bus or train? Who would be the best person to help if a child became detached from the group on a class visit to a zoo, park, shopping centre, market, sports event or street parade? Problem solving questions and practice are essential because, without practice, children remember the safe response to one situation and imagine that it will serve them in all situations.

School staff and parents should be invited to discuss how they can help children to gain independence while staying safe. For instance, when children only know about dangerous strangers, they trust anyone who refers to them by name. It follows that we increase their vulnerability to dangerous strangers when we adopt the common practice of attaching visible, personal name tags to children on class excursions and school open days.

DISCUSS SAFETY WITH BABYSITTERS

Parents should be alerted to the need for special care in the selection of babysitters. Parents are advised not to use male adolescents if this can be avoided. There are obvious risks in using young people who are at the stage of development where they may experience strong sexual curiosity and sexual urges without necessarily having healthy sexual outlets for their expression.

When parents leave children with others, they should *never* say, 'Be a good boy/girl and do what .... (the babysitter) says' because if that person is a molester, obedient children will obey all instructions.

To increase safety, parents should investigate their babysitter's reputation very carefully. Were previous clients satisfied? Did the children like them? Whenever possible, children should be introduced to new babysitters before they are employed so that parents can observe their interactions. If children feel uneasy with a new babysitter, parents must respect their intuition.

When parents leave children with others, they should give the children their contact telephone numbers so that they can call them if they are worried about something important. Babysitters (irrespective of their relationship to the parents) should also be told, in subtle ways, that children in the family do not keep secrets.

Sometimes children look unhappy because they don't like being left with other people. Sometimes, they are unhappy because they don't like their minders. Some children have very good reasons for being fearful.

When parents are aware of the risks, some respond by depriving themselves of a social life. This is harmful for family relationships and quite unnecessary. The answer is to provide the best possible personal safety information for children along with opportunities to practise assertiveness and independence.

DISCUSS HOW PARENTS CAN IMPROVE THEIR SUPPORT FOR CHILDREN

Parents inadvertently make it easy for child molesters to gain access to their children. Boys are given more freedom than girls and parents tend to assume that adults who 'get on well with kids' are safe and trustworthy people. Parents do not listen when children complain that they no longer want to go to scout meetings, boys' camps or visit grandad or stay with Uncle Jack. They do not ask the right questions because they are not expecting abuse to happen in their families.

If parents want their children to stay safe, they have to help them to stop unwanted touching within the family. It is easy enough for a parent to explain to a relative that the child is growing up and no longer likes being kissed or tickled. This gives the child two positive messages: first, that his or her feelings count and, second, that he/she can rely on parents to be supportive when adult touching is unwanted. Unfortunately, parents are least likely to support children's wishes when their own kisses, touching and tickling are unwanted.

Parents need to know that, to teach children to reject unwanted touching and make that teaching effective, we have to practise what we teach; there is no other way. To empower children, we may have to make changes to our own entrenched attitudes. In workshops, parents can be helped to work out what those attitudes are.

4 Developing Curriculum
Suggestions for Developing Safety and Personal Development Curriculum for Children with Disabilities Using an Integrated Approach

Level 1: Teach self help-skills

- Toileting.
- Dressing and grooming.
- Eating.
- Personal hygiene.

Level 2: Safety and self-protection

- Learn/practise safety rules with electricity, water, fire, medicines, drugs, traffic.
- Demonstrate safe behaviour.
- Identify and avoid potentially unsafe situations.
- Learn how to get help from adults when help is needed.
- Develop and practise problem solving skills.
- Develop accurate reporting skills.

Develop an active and healthy lifestyle

- Respect and use the correct names for sexual parts of the body.
- Learn the basics about how our bodies work, including genitals.
- Demonstrate confidence in personal and physical abilities.
- Respecting and caring for each other.

Self and relationships with others

- Identify own gender and the gender of others.
- Understand and identify feelings and learn to express them in appropriate ways.
- Identify safe behaviours to prevent or stop harassment or abuse.

- Display safe and appropriate behaviours with members of both sexes.
- Understand differences and similarities in people.
- Develop social skills.
- Understand personal space and respect the space of others.
- Develop communication skills.
- Learn new rules about keeping secrets.

Level 3: Safety and self-protection

- Help to formulate class and school rules and consequences.
- Identify consequences of unsafe behaviour.
- Learn to take responsibility for personal safety and self-protection.
- Learn own address and telephone number to access help.
- Learn to assert rights and take responsibility for own and others' safety and protection.
- Recognize the difference between assertiveness and aggression.
- Understand the consequences and responsibilities associated with sexual behaviour.
- Learn about helping and emergency services relating to child protection and disability.

Challenges for parents and teachers in developing safety skills with disabled children

There are many challenges for parents and teachers who introduce personal safety skills to children with disabilities. Some are listed below. This list should not be regarded as finite, however. Disabled children may have:

- learned to comply passively with all adult demands (especially those of care-givers)
- developed a poor body image and poor concepts relating to personal space, increasing their vulnerability to abuse
- no knowledge of their personal rights
- been sexually abused or acquired faulty knowledge (or no knowledge) about sexuality
- few opportunities for independence
- feelings of shame, guilt, low self-esteem, confusion, all of which increase their vulnerability to abusers who pretend to love them
- over-protective family members who do everything for them, depriving them of opportunities to assert themselves and gain independence.

(Meadow, 1980; Mindel and Vernon, 1987).

Parents and teachers should not underestimate the difficulties involved in teaching safety concepts to children with disabilities. Intellectually disabled children take their concepts of what is safe and unsafe or right and wrong from those in authority. Children turn to adults for guidance on safety issues. If adults say, 'It's all right.

There's nothing wrong', children tend to accept those assurances irrespective of whether they like or dislike what is happening.

An additional hazard is that, for both young and intellectually disabled children, moral judgements are dichotomous. They judge the outcomes and consequences of adult behaviour as 'good' or 'bad'. They then attribute dispositions of character to the adults based on those judgements. Adults engaged in abusive behaviour are judged according to how the outcomes are perceived; for example, when abusers present their victims with gifts (which are viewed as 'good' outcomes) the donors are perceived as 'good' people, irrespective of the sexual violation. Young children and those with developmental disabilities are incapable of judging adult motives, and collusion between an offender and an accomplice is beyond their comprehension. This again demonstrates the need for children to have practice in assessing situations rather than people.

Emotionally deprived children and those with intellectual disabilities are made more vulnerable by their desire to please and be accepted. Furthermore, young and intellectually disabled children cannot conceive that caregivers might do bad things to them.

Teachers and parents embarking on personal safety education should remember that some children may have already experienced sexual abuse without realizing that it was wrong. Most sexual misbehaviour initiated by caregivers contains mixed and incongruent messages: intrusive sexual contact can be confusing when it is accompanied by affectionate expressions. Gentle, non-intrusive contact can be followed by frightening threats and pressures for secrecy. In these inconsistent situations, children are unable to assess the intent and motivation of adults.

Children who attend special schools or units are likely to come from a wide range of cultures and socio-economic environments. Considerable diversity exists in any school group and teachers must be sensitive to these differences.

Additional challenges when working with children with developmental disabilities

- The concepts of 'stranger', 'unsafe' and sexual misbehaviour may be difficult to grasp and require thorough exploration using a variety of means.

- Young and intellectually disabled children tend to be 'doers'. They need a variety of concrete activities and they respond especially well to role plays and puppetry. Reinforcement must be ongoing.

- Intellectually disabled and young children may find it difficult to transfer information from one setting to another. For example, if taught to go to a safety house for help, children will suggest the safety house as the safe solution to all problems, even to the problem of being lost in a department store, at the beach, park or market. This means that concepts must be taught and reinforced in many different ways with ample time for revision. Parents and teachers should check children's learning after each session by asking relevant 'What if...?' questions.

- Instructions and questions must be clear. Use short, simple sentences. Avoid using either/or questions and those which can be answered with 'Yes' or 'No'. Ask one question at a time.

- Remember that intellectually disabled children have a much slower rate of progress than non disabled children of the same age. Information must be broken down into small segments and opportunities for practice must be provided on a daily basis (Anderson, 1982).

- Young children and intellectually disabled children are unlikely to grasp vague hints about unacceptable, sexual touching.

In addition, special attention must be given to developing children's social awareness and social interactions to reduce their vulnerability to abuse.

Additional challenges when working with deaf children

Studies show that the incidence of sexual abuse is much higher in the deaf child population than in the hearing population. Successful programs ensure that the following are addressed:

- The low status and devaluation of deaf people in education and society.

- The differences between the perceived and the actual vulnerability of children with hearing impairments to sexual abuse.

- Communication barriers between deaf family members and hearing school personnel. Some schools have found that the best teachers for personal safety programs are deaf teachers who can present material from a 'non-hearing' perspective.

- Mixed hearing and deaf teachers are desirable for all workshops.

- Deaf teachers need sensitive training to teach personal safety skills, bearing in mind that many members of the adult deaf population are also survivors of abuse.

- Children in special units or residential schools often live in far flung communities and parents may have little involvement with school programs.

- Because learning is predominantly visual, visual materials (such as pictorial cards, puppet shows, role plays and, if possible, special videos) should be used to extend and reinforce children's learning

- Inadequate supervision has been cited as a factor in the sexual abuse of children in residential schools (Sullivan, Vernon and Scanlan, 1987).

- Deaf and non verbal children often lack the means to communicate concerns about their bodies.

- Deaf children and deaf adults are denied knowledge, resources, communication skills and, as a result, may lack power in everyday life.

- In the deaf community, traditional notions of male–female roles still prevail. Strict adherence to sex role stereotypes is part of the social ideology that fosters abuse (Sanford, 1980).

Teaching personal safety skills to deaf children requires a heightened awareness of the varied communication backgrounds of individual children whose access to communication has been restricted. Few deaf children are likely to have had the opportunity to discuss sensitive sexual issues with reliable adults. Because shared communication is essential to the establishment of trust, extra care must be taken to create clear, open and safe communications between teachers, parents and children.

To adapt a personal safety program for use with deaf children, we have to go beyond the translation of the text from print to sign language and change the perspective to a visual one. Well-intentioned hearing professionals often select signs and ways of presenting information that do not relate to the ways in which children view things. Children who have a comparatively good knowledge of

English often miss the subtleties of detail and innuendo that are used in oral presentations. Teachers must examine the content carefully and, if necessary, 're-vamp' it to a more visual 'mind set' that will meet the needs of the group to be taught.

Young children often try to make sense of learning experiences by acting them out. When they have experienced surgery in hospital, they play at nurses and doctors until the experience becomes less troublesome. As visual learners, children with hearing impairments may repeat behaviour witnessed on television. Typically, they miss or misconstrue the discussion that accompanies the pictures and when adults respond negatively they learn that the behaviour is not acceptable. Deaf children are often punished for unacceptable behaviour which they do not understand. They feel shame and guilt but, because the unacceptability is not explained to them, they have no opportunity to learn from the experience.

The most efficient teaching methods always involve children's participation. However, we must bear in mind that there is a much higher tolerance of touch in the deaf community than in the hearing community. Touching is essential for attracting attention and transmitting information. Hugs and other touches are commonly involved in communicative interaction between deaf people. As a result, the acceptability of certain touching behaviours may be different in children with hearing impairments. The differences between acceptable and unacceptable touching must be clearly illustrated and explained. This can be conveyed by using pictures, puppets, role plays accompanied by subtle changes of facial expression and body movement to demonstrate unacceptable and 'yukky' touching.

When using role plays, the circumstances should be relevant to the children. For example, 'offenders' should include both hearing and deaf people. Potential helpers should also represent both categories. Discussion should explore the possibilities of offenders using sign language or oral communications.

Adapting programs for children who have hearing impairments

Some children now have technical aids which give them access to telephones. However, deaf and non verbal children may not be aware of resources such as Rape Crisis and telephone help lines and, without the help of a child protection program, few parents realize the need for that kind of information.

An additional hazard for parents and children is the lack of specialist treatment facilities for victims of abuse who have communication problems. The school is often left in the unsatisfactory situation of having to provide therapy under the guidance of other professionals. Before programs are introduced, the personnel responsible for children with hearing impairments should locate professionals or agencies that are capable of providing therapy for them. They should create support networks *before* cases of abuse are reported. If no support workers are available, schools and parents should contact their child protection authorities and lobby local politicians and media.

All children with hearing impairments benefit from opportunities to practise yelling and saying 'No'. They are often told that their voices sound funny and they may be reluctant to try a new form of guttural yell. They will need to use tactile–kinaesthetic cues to differentiate the new yell from the one formed in the larynx. In common with intellectually disabled and non verbal children, they also need to be taught when and how to use other attention seeking strategies such as pulling alarms on trains, stopping buses, triggering fire alarms and writing simple requests for help. In addition, physical defence training is an important asset for all children with disabilities.

Most parents are concerned about the safety risks to children resulting from their deficiencies in communication. Hearing parents may try to counter these risks by over restricting children, reducing their opportunities for independence. Safety concepts may be new to their children. It will be necessary to explain all the vocabulary words using a variety of signs and examples until there is evidence that the message has been conveyed. Allow children to show you the signs that they use for body parts and sexual touches and use them whenever possible. If we use children's language and suggestions, we facilitate communication and reduce feelings of discomfort (Kennedy, 1989; Mounty and Fetterman, 1989).

Working with non verbal children

When working with non verbal children, it is advisable to consult a speech pathologist for the acquisition and use of the appropriate Blissymbols, Picture Communication Symbols (PCS) (Mayer-Johnson Co.), Picture Vocabulary System for Sexuality (BC Rehabilitation Society) or similar symbol system.

When working with children who have visual impairments

Children with severe visual impairments are likely to need extra help to develop body awareness. This is necessary to teach safe social behaviours that provide protection from the risk of abuse. Anatomically correct dolls with genitals, mouth, anus and breasts are a 'must' for sightless children. Dolls should be selected for their realistic 'feel'. Again, it is useful to involve an adult with impaired sight to ensure that teachers provide the appropriate cultural perspectives.

When working with children with severe physical disabilities

Developing safety skills in children with severe physical disabilities involves a focus on ways of increasing independence, especially in matters relating to hygiene, the development of confidence and self-esteem and the identification of appropriate and inappropriate touching. The latter is especially important for children who depend on others for personal care.

Provide curriculum to develop self-esteem

To keep children safe, we have to give them the knowledge, skills and confidence to reject sexual misbehaviour involving bigger, stronger and more powerful people. Developing a positive self-image is at the root of all confidence building and self-protection. Because of society's high valuation of physical perfection, it is difficult for disabled youngsters to acquire a healthy level of self-esteem. Furthermore, young people with severe physical disabilities have few opportunities to gain achievements of the kind that bring personal satisfaction. Curriculum planning must take this into account.

Our self-esteem is affected by how we are treated by others. We judge ourselves by the way people behave towards us. When children are treated as helpless and hopeless, they view themselves as helpless and hopeless. Negative messages are transmitted by body language, especially facial expression and tone of voice. Comments such as, 'Here, let me do it...you make such a mess...it's quicker if I do it', ensure that children stop making an effort and become resigned to dependency. Some teachers, caregivers and families are reluctant to let disabled children gain independence. The reasons for this should be discussed thoroughly at staff and parent meetings.

Devaluing attitudes leave disabled young people with the notion that they have no control over what happens to them. This results in a victim's attitude to life which, in turn, increases their vulnerability to abuse.

In some cases, it may be necessary to help children and adolescents to overcome feelings of powerlessness at an individual level before they can be taught the skills necessary for self-protection and personal safety.

Schools, institutions, families and children should work together to provide an integrated approach to independence and protection. Home–school cooperation is vital but may be difficult to obtain when children travel by special transport and there is little parent–teacher contact.

Children's learning can best be achieved with a three-pronged approach incorporating:

- **Curriculum for self-development:** providing,
    - opportunities for the development of a positive self image
    - opportunities to practise decision making skills
    - help for children to manage emotions and handle conflict
    - help for children to cope with grief and loss
    - opportunities for children to learn about their developing sexuality, rights and responsibilities
    - a positive learning environment which caters for individual differences and needs
    - opportunities to develop children's curiosity and information seeking skills using their own experience and interests.

- **Curriculum to develop relationship skills:** by,
    - improving communication skills
    - teaching and encouraging the practice of assertiveness skills
    - giving and receiving feedback
    - learning to give, seek and reject help
    - helping children to manage conflict in relationships
    - helping children to create and end relationships.

- **Curriculum for life skills:** including,
    - teaching self care, health and hygiene management, mobility skills, home management, meal preparation, leisure skills, preparation for employment and use of public services. (Adapted from suggestions by Fenton and Hughes, 1989)

Help children to develop independence

The task of teaching personal safety skills to disabled children may appear daunting. It can be achieved if parents and school personnel are trained in child protection and work together to develop children's self-esteem, confidence, assertiveness and independence and provide the necessary information about body rights. One problem is that most parents try to protect disabled children by exercising total control over their lives. Over-protection has the opposite effect to the one desired. Children's dependence and ignorance make them more vulnerable to abuse and they have no idea what to do when things go wrong. Parents indoctrinated with the myth of the dangerous stranger believe, mistakenly, that if they act as taxi drivers for children they will be safe (Briggs, 1987). It rarely occurs to them that their children might be unsafe in school, church or even in the next room in the company of a friend. Sexual offenders are audacious. Offences sometimes take place while parents are in the same room. In general, the more bizarre and daring the offences, the less likely that victims are believed.

When children rely on others for getting in and out of bed, dressing, showering, changing sanitary pads and toileting, staff and parents should explore opportunities to increase self-reliance. Unfortunately, adults often do things for children because they are slow and messy and adult intervention is faster and, in the short term, easier. This is especially likely to happen when adults are caring for several children and have a busy schedule.

Opportunities for independence and achievement are necessary for the development of social skills and a positive self-image. The Royal Association for Disability and Rehabilitation found that disabled young people are deprived of information, especially information concerning their own disabilities, their rights and the services that exist to help them (RADAR, 1989). It was suggested that these issues should be explored and addressed in school programs with the twin aims of increasing children's self-esteem and independence.

The keys to independence are choice and privacy. Some disabled children are deprived of even the most elementary choices. They are well fed and well dressed but they cannot choose what they eat or wear. They are not even allowed to select the flavours of their drinks or ice-creams. When children are severely disabled, they are often assumed to be insensitive. They are deprived of opportunities for privacy, including privacy for their most intimate tasks. This has to be rectified if we aim to develop personal safety skills.

Barriers to independent living can be summarized as follows:

- Negative societal attitudes towards people with disabilities. In the past, cultural and religious doctrines associated disability with evil, fear, ugliness and the punishment of mothers for wrong doing.

- Societal ignorance of how to relate to people with disabilities.

- Pity for the disabled person.

- Intrusive curiosity or benevolence.

In addition, low self-esteem and lack of confidence, in turn, prevent children from asserting and protecting themselves when they face potentially dangerous situations.

The first task for teachers and caregivers is, then, to explore their own attitudes to the disabled. The second task is to plan and implement curriculum that will help children to become more independent. This curriculum must, of necessity, involve parent participation.

Self care is vital for self-esteem and self-protection

Self care is vital for independence, self-esteem and self-protection. Self care is especially important for children with developmental disabilities. Intervention should start at preschool with therapists, parents, staff and children working together. Whenever possible, children should be taught to bath, shower and shampoo their hair unaided. They should be taught how to select, change and launder personal clothing and bedding. Adolescent females need to learn when and how to change sanitary protection and use hygienic methods of disposal. Both boys and girls are likely to need counselling and guidance on their sexual development. It is sometimes necessary to tell children that masturbation is 'OK' but we don't do it in public; we go to our bedroom or bathroom and do it in privacy with the door closed.

Children in social isolation are likely to acquire inaccurate information on sexual matters from their peers. Disabled adolescents have to be taught that they have responsibilities as well as rights in their sexual relationships. They have to be taught what is and is not socially acceptable behaviour. This is especially necessary when working with intellectually disabled males who have adult sexual urges but are not at an adult intellectual level. Male and female victims of sexual abuse are at risk of repeating their emotionally disturbing sexual experiences with younger children especially if their own cries for help have been ignored.

Children with severe visual impairments are often confused by demands for modesty. They refuse to conform to societal rules about closing bedroom and toilet doors. They argue that 'Everyone uses a toilet so why the fuss about closing the door?' They see themselves as asexual, ridiculing societal taboos and adult concerns. In addition, those who have a poor self-image often engage in risky behaviour, telling themselves that no one would want to have sex with them because their bodies are defective.

It is important to encourage personal care to develop a positive body image. Teachers should draw attention to the things that children do well rather than things that they do badly. Children need encouragement for effort as well as for achievement.

Many severely disabled children have to tolerate staff touching parts of their bodies that would not be permitted in non disabled society. The goals of personal care assistants must be to provide the necessary help while respecting young people's privacy. Many are highly embarrassed by their own helplessness. When young people need help that involves touching them in intimate places, they should be asked, 'Do you want me to do this for you?' providing the opportunity for children to say 'No! I want to do it myself'.

Some professionals show resentment when requested to change long established practices by asking for the child's permission to conduct internal medical examinations.

The sexuality of young people must be acknowledged and respected if we want adolescents to respect the sexuality of others. Staff are rarely taught to cope with their own negative feelings about disability when they handle children with disabilities. Feelings of discomfort and embarrassment are quickly transmitted to the children they are there to help.

In any education program, all children should have opportunities to improve their health and fitness, especially when they use wheelchairs or have limited mobility. Exercise is essential and a lack of it decreases mobility. Class activities should enable children to participate at their own level. Goals should be set to beat their own previous best performances so that success is achievable. Parents who say emphatically that they want their children to have a normal education are often terrified when their children participate in sports. Parents are likely to be even more afraid when children become involved in mobility training and are taught to go into city centres, use public transport, transfer from wheelchair to taxi and negotiate obstacles.

We can see how the greatest obstacles to independence and self-protection can be the caring parents who over-protect their children and discourage independent activities.

Developing social awareness and appropriate social interactions in children with intellectual disabilities

Some of the behaviours to be encouraged and practised are:

- standing at an appropriate distance from others when in conversation
- establishing appropriate visual contact
- using appropriate language and topics of conversation
- demonstrating a range of acceptable self care procedures in different environments, for example, finding and using a public toilet and washing hands
- knowing the full range of touches and in what circumstances it is appropriate to use them: for example when to shake hands, who or what to hug, kiss, cuddle, stroke, tickle[1]
- demonstrate appropriate behaviour when rejecting friendship or intimacy.

Children should be taught life skills so that they can use initiative in different situations such as:

- ordering, paying for and eating a snack
- making a complaint when something is unsatisfactory; coping with teasing by non disabled adolescents
- buying personal toiletries from a shop
- travelling alone by public transport (for example, how to choose a seat, how to decide where to sit if the bus is nearly full, who to talk to and what to talk about on the bus or at the bus stop. When is it all right to talk to the bus driver? What do you do if you catch the wrong bus or forget to get off at your bus stop? Is it all right to stare at someone? When is it all right to give your name and address?)

Help children to understand what topics of conversation are acceptable and unacceptable in different circumstances.

Make provision for children to work at their own pace

Please allow participants to work at their own individual pace, taking as long as necessary to develop each concept. With developmentally disabled children, it may be necessary to repeat the same session, with slight variations, several times and in different ways until children show that they are capable of transferring safety knowledge to different hypothetical situations. Some ideas are extremely difficult

---

1   Some children may need to be taught that it is unacceptable to scratch or rub their genitals in public (but they can do it as often as they like when alone in the privacy of their own room, toilet or locked bathroom).

to grasp. Those who have a poor body image and those trained to be compliant will require much more repetition and practice than those who have achieved a high degree of independence.

Maintain regular contact with parents to keep them informed about children's progress. When appropriate, send children's completed workshops home so that parents can see for themselves what their children are doing.

Group work

- In general, the smaller the group, the better.
- It is important that sessions are held in a quiet and comfortable place where the group will not be interrupted.
- If possible, the class teacher should have a co-group leader or assistant.
- Seat the children in a circle so that each person has eye-to-eye contact with the teacher or group leader and other class members.
- Use 'warm up' exercises at the beginning of each session to encourage children to participate and focus on 'self'. For example, sing and do actions to songs such as, 'Hokey Cokey' and get children to establish their own personal space. Sing the song, 'My body'.
- Establish a set of group rules at the beginning of the program in consultation with the children, such as:
    - we listen to and show respect for what each person has to say
    - we agree to take turns in talking
    - no teasing or telling tales to others about what was said in the group
    - we all have the option to 'pass' or leave the group if we feel uncomfortable.
- De-brief the children at the end of each session by referring to group rules, emphasizing that if group members wish to talk to leaders privately between sessions, they may do so.

When working with groups, please ensure that each child has the opportunity to contribute to discussion. Care should be taken that sessions are not monopolized by the most confident, articulate members. Questions should be addressed to specific children rather than to the group as a whole.

Develop children's problem solving skills

We cannot prepare children for every dangerous situation that they will encounter. They have the best chance of staying safe, however, if they can think of a range of possible solutions and choose the safest. This is a skill that is only learned by practice. The following hints are provided for helping children to develop problem solving skills.

- Identify a problem that is relevant to the children.
- Frame questions around the problem and ask, 'What if someone'…(or)'Just suppose that someone…what could he/she do to stay safe?'
- Use a third party approach whenever possible: in presenting hypothetical problems for children to solve (especially problems relating to touching), it is recommended that puppets should be used as offenders and victims.

Questions then revolve around what victims could do to stay safe. A third party approach is essential for protecting children who may have already been abused.

- Use brainstorming methods to generate a list of possible strategies that could be used in the situation. If the children are new to brainstorming techniques, simple rules must be created for them, such as:

  - Everyone must be given the right to speak.
  - Only one suggestion may be given at a time.
  - Everyone's contribution will be respected and recorded.
  - Some secrets should be shared privately with a trusted person, rather than with the whole group.

The teacher will be available to talk to individual children about things that concern them at the end of every session. Parents and other family members should be recruited to provide practice in solving problems in and around home.

Develop children's assertiveness skills

It is important that children learn and have opportunities to practise assertiveness skills so that they can respond to potentially exploitive situations in a convincing way. For children to acquire safety skills, we need to go beyond cognitive learning and provide opportunities for children to translate their knowledge into safe behaviour through active participation and practice. As most children with disabilities have learned to be passive, this will necessitate changing their attitudes to change their behaviour.

Parents, teachers and caregivers are often afraid of giving children permission to say 'No' in case they say 'No' to them. Compliant children are easier to handle than those who express their needs and feelings. Protective education for the adults should stress the reasons why children with disabilities need appropriate assertiveness skills.

'Suppose that your parents go out and a friend comes round to keep you company. As he's leaving, he falls and can't move. He says he thinks that he's broken his leg. What can you do?'

'Suppose that you got lost on a school excursion and you had no money left. How would you stay safe? Suppose that a lady saw that you had problems and offered to take you home. What would you say? Why? Would it be safe to go with her? What would be the safest thing to do?'

'Suppose that a big boy offers you some pills and says, "They're great! If you take them, you'll be able to do anything that you want to do. You'll feel really good. Let me give you one to try". What should you do? Why?'

'Suppose that you're being picked on by a bigger boy or girl at school. What could you do to stay safe?

'Suppose that you're out by yourself and you see a gang of rough looking big boys coming towards you. What could you do to stay safe?'

'Suppose that someone comes to sit by you on the bus and that person makes you feel uncomfortable. What could you do?'

'Suppose that someone dares you to drink beer/smoke marijuana/sniff powder or adhesives/steal something from a shop. What could you do? Why? Would that be safe? What else could you do?'

'Suppose that you're in a cinema with a friend. A man comes to sit in the next seat. When the lights go down, he puts his hand on your leg. What could you do?'

'Suppose that you get really scared when you are in the house (or bedroom) on your own in the dark. What could you do to make yourself feel safer?'

'Suppose that you are out shopping and a man suddenly puts his hand up your dress/down your pants. Is that allowed? What could you do?'

'Suppose that a man you know shows you dirty pictures. Should grown ups do that?

What should you do?'

Provide a positive learning environment

It is important for teachers and parents to work towards the growth of self-esteem in each individual child. The less confident, less articulate children can be encouraged by praising their efforts. When children are offering suggestions for safety, use supportive phrases, such as:

'Thank you for trying so hard. That was a difficult question'.

'Well done! Now, can you think of something else...?'

'You have some good ideas there. What else could you do?'

Sometimes, children will make silly, unsafe responses. Boys with severe physical disabilities who come from violent homes and/or spend a large part of their time watching violent movies and video games are the ones most likely to offer violent answers to everyday safety problems, for example:

'If I got home to a locked house, I'd smash a window and climb in'.

'If someone gave me a sloppy kiss, I'd stab them to death'.

When children make bizarre suggestions, take care that others do not ridicule them. Invite the contributors to suggest possible consequences of their proposed actions. Thank them for trying but ask, 'Would that be safe? What might happen? What else could happen? Now...tell me what you could do that would be safer'.

If foolishness persists, give a stern reminder that 'We are here to learn about staying safe. Now, please try again'. Draw attention to rules as necessary. When children say that they cannot think of a solution to a problem, draw them in gradually with, 'Just suppose that... Would that be safe? Now, if she... Would that be even safer? What else could she do?'

An alternative is to use the, 'Let's pretend that you do know' approach. This usually results in a smile and an attempted response.

Interrupt disclosures of a personal nature

When children feel safe in a group, they sometimes expose themselves to public humiliation by disclosing personal information about family fights or sexual abuse. An adolescent girl accidentally revealed that she was a lifelong victim of father–daughter incest. She hated her father's behaviour but, until that moment, had not realized that it was wrong. The group response was one of shocked incredulity:

'You must be joking!'...'You must be stupid!'...'Yuk! How can you do that with your father?' Unsupportive responses are psychologically damaging and children who accidentally disclose sexual abuse are at risk of losing what is left of their self-esteem.

Some disclosures are unpredictable. In a discussion on 'Pets', a seven-year-old child told the class, 'I have a dog. My dog has sex with me in my bed at night'. The student teacher smiled, thanked the child for her input, moved on to the next respondent and waited for an opportune, private moment to investigate whether she had understood the child correctly.

Be ready to interrupt and protect children from disclosing sensitive information about themselves or their families. Say, 'I'm glad that you want to tell me about this. It's very important and I want to hear it. Can we talk about it in a few minutes? Just the two of us? Right now, we must finish...'(bringing the child back to the job in hand).

Ensure that the child is taken to a quiet, comfortable, private place to continue the conversation.

Teach children how to stay safe

o   Inform children about the helping services.

It may be useful for older children to meet professionals involved in child protection and other helping services so that they know who to contact if they need help. Police officers and social workers who have an interest in children with disabilities might be willing to talk to a small group of young people about their work in child protection. School counsellors and school nurses should be invited to tell children about their jobs and how they can help children. It is also important that children are put in contact with services catering specifically for their disability group.

o   Ensure that all class members are capable of making emergency and collect (reverse charge) telephone calls.

Help children to learn about what an emergency is. Teach children how to report emergencies to police, fire and ambulance services. Ensure that they know the circumstances in which the services should be used. What might happen if someone sent for the Fire Brigade when there wasn't a fire? Take children to public telephones to ensure that they can use them.

Institutions should have public phones available for children's use, i.e. situated at an appropriate height for children in wheelchairs. This is especially important for establishments with residential facilities. It is often argued that children with disabilities are disadvantaged by their lack of access to telephone communications. In a real emergency, they often do not know what to do.

Provide opportunities for children to practise making decisions

Because children with disabilities have few opportunities for decision making, it is important that schools provide choices in the curriculum.

Teachers can:

•   give children a selection of activities from which to choose

•   encourage children to provide reasons for their decisions

- use a contract system in which children make a commitment to the completion of specific tasks of their own choice
- use learning centres which provide a variety of learning experience
- give children a list of themes or topics from which they can choose
- let children take turns to choose stories or songs
- give children a wide range of materials for creative activities
- help to make children responsible for their own behaviour.

When children behave badly, encourage them to express how they feel and why they are upset. Help them to realize that they have choices in what they do. If they choose to behave in an anti-social way, they must be helped to understand the likely consequences: 'What might happen if you do that? Then, what might happen? How will everyone else feel? Is that what you really want? What would you really like to happen?'

If children have been debarred from playing in a specific area because of misbehaviour, they should be involved, after a reasonable period of time, in deciding when they are ready to return and comply with the rules. It helps, of course, if teachers involve children in deciding what the rules are, why they are needed and what penalties might be appropriate for rule-breakers. Caution is advised however because children frequently want to adopt very harsh penalties for infringements by other people.

Teach children how to communicate effectively

When children with disabilities need help, they are often disadvantaged by poor communication skills. It will be beneficial if they can be taught how to:

- talk, listen and look at people, establishing eye contact without staring
- practise using an appropriate posture and stand at a suitable distance from those with whom they are communicating, i.e. neither too close nor too distant
- use clear firm speech for communicating serious issues: children with intellectual disabilities often have speech difficulties
- interrupt a conversation politely to disclose an emergency.

This is a difficult challenge when working with children who have severe intellectual disabilities. Augmented communication strategies can help although the problem is often as much conceptual as one of communication.

Use role plays

Whenever appropriate, role play situations should be used to reinforce learning. Children with intellectual disabilities learn safety skills very effectively through role plays (Anderson, 1982). Children can be used to act out scenes involving bullying or unwanted touches of a non sexual nature. One person takes the part of the perpetrator and another person acts as the victim. Children can also role play scenes involving tricks by potentially dangerous strangers. Participation should be limited to about five minutes.

The teacher can act as a coach, stopping proceedings at appropriate moments to ask participants how they felt about what had just taken place. Teachers encourage the promotion of children's own ideas for role play after the discussion of a particular safety issue. Primary and secondary school children will have plenty of ideas but they may need guidance relating to their appropriateness. The capacity for role play may be very limited in a group of children with profound intellectual disabilities. Scenes should be frozen at crucial points to enable children to suggest how participants feel and what they could do for bad feelings to stop. Brainstorming methods should be used to enable children to put forward their own ideas for staying safe. The coach may stop proceedings to ask the audience to help victims who are uncertain about what they should do. The coach uses positive reinforcement for each appropriate example of assertiveness.

To avoid confusion, group members should be instructed to raise their hands when they wish to ask questions. Children benefit from both participating in and watching role plays. They can be a very effective learning tool for those who need a lot of different opportunities to explore the various concepts.

Role play offers an excellent technique for children with disabilities to learn and practise assertiveness skills. Children act out roles in given and imaginary situations. Members of the audience offer suggestions, comments and encouragement. The rules for role play include:

- concentrating on the roles
- trying not to be distracted
- being good listeners and observers
- making, receiving and trying out suggestions for more assertive (safe) behaviour
- having fun while learning.

To demonstrate inappropriate touching, use puppets, dolls or suitable pictures.

5 Responding to the Actual or Suspected Sexual Abuse of Children

When children disclose information relating to sexual abuse we should:

- Put our own feelings aside and take care not to show that we are shocked, disgusted or embarrassed. Expressions of horror or disbelief will freeze the conversation. The most helpful response is one that is supportive and calm, giving the impression that we hear these kinds of disclosures daily.

- Try to protect victims from disclosing details of abuse in public. If possible, ask someone to take care of other children so that you can continue the conversation in privacy.

- Say, 'I'm really pleased that you told me… It must have been worrying for you… I'm so sorry that this happened to you… Grown-ups know that they aren't allowed to do that to kids. Unfortunately, it's happened to lots of children in this school… It shouldn't happen and I want to help'.

- Never blame victims or make judgements about what happened.

- Never ask questions that could make victims feel guilty or inadequate (such as, 'Why didn't you tell me earlier?', 'Why didn't you say "No"?' 'Haven't we told you not to talk to strangers?' 'You know you aren't allowed to come home that way.' 'Are you sure that's what really happened? I don't believe it!')

- Report *suspicions* of abuse to child protection authorities; it is their job to investigate whether abuse actually occurred.

- Inform children who disclose abuse that it will be necessary to tell a social worker because we must all try to stop adults from doing this to kids.

- Tell children about what happens once abuse is reported.

- Arrange for victims to see suitably qualified and experienced therapists or help parents to make the arrangements.

- Help parents to make contact with a parent support group.

When disclosures involve deaf and non verbal children

When reporting suspicions of sexual abuse involving deaf and non-verbal children, staff should request the child protection agency to employ the services of a qualified and suitably experienced interpreter. Problems arise when interviewers are inexperienced in translating information relating to sexual offences, feel uncomfortable with the subject and/or fail to gain the victim's trust. Children may feel more comfortable if the trusted staff member who received the report works in tandem with the interviewers. This is useful when assessment is urgent or when the interviewee has intellectual disabilities, multiple disabilities or a very idiosyncratic communication system which strangers may not understand.

Investigate suspicions

Teachers often have 'gut feelings' that children have been abused but they are frustrated by a lack of concrete evidence. 'Gut feelings' are the result of many disconnected observations which come together over a period of time. Teachers are often reluctant to investigate hunches because they 'don't know what to say' and are frightened of 'putting ideas into children's heads'.

When we experience these feelings, we should express our concern for the wellbeing of the child on the lines of,

> 'I'm really worried about you. You haven't been yourself lately. I don't like to see you looking so sad. I know that something is bothering you. Is it something or somebody? Is it at home or at school? Can you tell me about it? Why not? Is it a secret? Is it a good secret or a bad secret? Who else knows the secret? What will happen if you tell me? Who said so?'

These kinds of questions are the ones most likely to produce the required information without asking a child to break the secret. If children have not undertaken a personal safety program which tells them which secrets to keep and which to tell, it is important to teach them that we don't have to keep bad or yukky secrets. When children show signs of emotional disturbance and indicate that they are angry with certain people, we can ask questions such as,

> 'You seem to be angry with...
>
> Let's talk about it. Can you tell me what happened to upset you...
>
> Why can't you tell me? Is it hard to talk about? Is it a secret?
>
> (Continue as before)...
>
> Has he/she touched you in a way that you don't like?
>
> Did you have to touch him/her in a way that you didn't like?...
>
> (*Gently*) Can you point to where he/she touched you?
>
> (*or*) Maybe you can point to the place on this doll (or picture)'.

Always use language that is appropriate for the child's developmental level. Ask children to tell you the names that they use for their genitals and use their vocabulary.

Use open questions

To avoid the possible contamination of children's evidence, try to use open, not closed questions which restrict answers to 'Yes' or 'No'.

Open questions allow for a range of possible answers. For example, ask, 'Show me where he touches you', *not* 'Does he touch you between your legs?' When abuse is suspected make an immediate record of what happened, what questions were asked and how children responded.

When the accused is a juvenile

Sexual offences by juveniles should be reported and taken as seriously as offences by adults. They can be just as damaging. Sexual abuse is habitual and it is important that juvenile perpetrators receive therapeutic help to reduce the likelihood that they will become lifelong offenders.

Report the facts

Where there is a reasonable suspicion that sexual abuse has occurred, the facts should be reported directly to the statutory child protection services. **Never inform the victim's parents directly:** that is the social worker's job. If you inform parents first, they may challenge and forewarn the offender or, if a trusted family member is involved, they may persuade the child to withdraw the allegation.

Staff in schools and residential institutions have an obligation to get to know their local child protection workers and create supportive relationships with individuals who can be trusted to respond sensitively to the sexual abuse of children with disabilities. If immediate action is required to prevent the abuser from escaping detection, police should be called. When police have to interview a child, it is best to request an officer who has expertise in handling offences against children with special needs.

Assure the child that reporting is right

It is important to let child victims know that they did the right thing by talking about the abuse. They need frequent assurance that children are never to blame for what grown-ups do. If secrecy was involved, explain that offenders use secrets because they know they are doing wrong. They ask children to keep secrets because they are scared of getting into trouble. Children know that this happens in their peer group but they are seldom aware that adults use the same strategies.

The assessment process

After a report has been made, the victim should be questioned in detail by social workers and police. There may be a medical assessment by a paediatrician and a psychological assessment by a child psychologist who has specialist skills in this work. If charges are laid, the child will also be interviewed by the prosecuting lawyer.

Each of the professionals has a different priority. Children must be reassured that it is all right to tell these people about what happened because they are there to help.

It is important to make interviewers aware of children's different levels of understanding, communicative abilities and special needs before interviews take place. Children should also have the choice of a support person or interpreter to be present at the interview. Parents should *never* be present because they find it difficult to conceal their feelings. Children then edit what they say, withholding the shocking detail and minimizing what happened to reduce the risk of causing distress. Investigators seldom hear the full story if parents are present.

Supporting parents

In some areas, there are organizations available to provide support for non-offending parents of sexually abused children through the assessment process and court proceedings. Support workers are usually parents who have been through the same trauma and survived. They assist family members to work through their own angry and confused feelings. Help of this kind is especially necessary when the abuse involves the betrayal of the parent's trust as well as the child's trust.

When groups are not available specifically for this purpose, parent counselling is usually available through parent support groups, Community and Women's Health Centres, Rape Crisis Centres and other social services. Teachers should make enquiries about local counselling facilities so that they can refer parents when necessary. Counselling is vital because, if parents do not work through their own feelings about the abuse, they are unlikely to be able to support their children in psychologically helpful ways.

Supporting the abused child

There are many ways in which teachers, caregivers and parents can support child victims of sexual abuse:

- Stay close to the child immediately after disclosure and provide a sense of physical security.
- Never promise to keep abuse secret. If a promise is made accidentally, the adult should explain to the child why offences must be reported.
- Respect the child's privacy. Disclosures should not be discussed in staff rooms or in the presence of others.
- Emphasize repeatedly that, no matter what children do they are never to blame for what bigger, stronger and older people do to them.
- Maintain a normal affectionate interaction with the child.
- Never promise that reporting abuse will guarantee the child's safety: no one can give that assurance.
- When victims look worried or sad, take them aside and confirm that they have had a very worrying time. Invite them to talk about what is worrying them at that moment.
- When victims behave aggressively, tell them that it is all right for them to feel angry. If possible, invite them to express their angry feelings. Provide therapeutic activities for the release of anger.
- Victims need extra support when they have to attend medical examinations, interviews or make court appearances which remind them of the abuse. Their behaviour is likely to regress immediately before and after these interviews and when they see the offender.

- If victims behave sexually, provide reassurance that they no longer have to do those things to please adults. Confirm that, 'safe hugs are available at any time'.

- Allow victims to think kindly of offenders if they previously enjoyed a rewarding relationship with them.

Information needed by child protection services when suspicions of abuse are reported

- Child's name, address and telephone number, gender, date of birth and school attended.

- Names and addresses and telephone numbers of parents and guardians.

- Names, addresses and occupations of suspected persons and their relationship to the victims.

- What the child said or did or what others said to cause the suspicions.

- Details of behavioural or other indicators including dates, times, frequency and circumstances.

- The current home or care situation of the victim, i.e. who lives where and with whom

- Other agencies involved with the family.

It is useful for institutions to provide incident reports for teachers so that they can (routinely) keep records of suspicious behaviours (See page 73 for sample).

Therapy for victims of sexual abuse

It is important that schools and residential institutions help all child victims to receive therapy following sexual abuse. It should be remembered that some children are very distressed by sexual touching on top of clothing. We cannot act as judges of victims' emotional reactions on the basis of our own perceptions of the gravity of offences.

Treatment is necessary to:

- alleviate the victim's feelings of guilt engendered by the abuser

- alleviate the non-offending parents' feelings of guilt

- explore victims' feelings about their disabilities: children think that they were abused *because* they are disabled. Do not try to convince them that they are wrong. Start with the child's reality, offering suggestions as to why abusers select children for sexual misbehaviour. The list will mention disability but in such a way that the problem is placed firmly with the offender (with no excuses). There is then no reason to postulate about why a particular child was chosen.

Explore issues of trust to help victims regain their trust in other people and themselves. Provide basic information about normal sexuality and interpersonal relationships; this is vital because victims have already learned about abnormal sexuality and if we do not teach them what is the normal range of appropriate behaviours, they cannot recognize the abnormal when they encounter it.

Discuss homosexual issues when necessary, assuring boys that they were chosen because they were children, not because they are effeminate, weak or homosexual. Boys are especially likely to worry about homosexuality if they enjoyed receiving genital stimulation and have no history of relating to girls. Without information, they often mistake the first ejaculation as the sign of serious illness, such as an internal abscess.

Homosexuality is one of the hardest topics for people to discuss when they have no experience of it. Irrespective of how parents, teachers or therapists feel, male victims must be given the opportunity to discuss these issues. In addition:

- talk about the dynamics of abuse to reduce the 'damaged goods syndrome'
- explore relationships and sexual relationships
- teach personal safety skills and inform children about their rights
- develop ways of communicating feelings
- encourage the development of supportive relationships
- encourage emotional independence, helping children to recognize and express emotions
- encourage the development and use of decision making skills to reduce reliance on others
- explore the issues of disability and victims' suspicions that they were abused because they were bad, abnormal and disabled
- explore and encourage a healthy release of angry feelings relating to the disability – anger can best be expressed to outside, independent therapists who can provide continuity of care
- work on issues relating to body image, the acceptance of the disability and the development of self-esteem and independence
- help victims to develop a personal value system, exploring inappropriate/appropriate values in relationships
- explore, eliminate and re-channel secondary behavioural characteristics such as inappropriate acting out of the sexual abuse, self-destructive behaviour and aggression
- reduce depression by helping victims to express their anger relating to their abuse, the abuser and the adults who did not protect them.

It is very difficult for an autistic child or a cerebral palsy child with limited speech and movement to express anger and other emotions that the non disabled can interpret. All too often, there is an assumption that because children have difficulty in expressing hostile feelings, there are no feelings present. Anger is always present after abuse. The therapist has to explore ways of releasing harmful feelings.

An additional difficulty for victims and therapists alike is that children with disabilities often lack an effective vocabulary to describe their feelings. They have 'good' and 'bad' and very little in between. They don't have 'depressed...frustrated...worried...' or the more precise and specific concepts that others might understand. Therapists and social workers need to find and fill the language gaps. It is useless to embark on special interviews or therapy without first investigating what vocabulary is present or absent.

Barriers to therapy

Without support and therapy, child victims of sexual abuse are at high risk of serious emotional disturbance which often results in the reproduction of the abusive behaviour with other children. The victim becomes the offender and another generation of child sexual abuse victims is created. Victims with disabilities are the ones least likely to be offered therapeutic help. There are various reasons for this.

Denial of responsibility by offenders

It is very hard for children to get help when offenders are members of their own tight social circle. The sense of powerlessness, already doubly present as a result of their childhood status and disability, is overwhelming when they become trapped in abusive relationships. When the offender is a relative, the victim is often given responsibility for keeping the family together. Similarly, when a member of staff is accused, others rally round to protect the adult. The victim is also expected to protect the adults who should be protecting them and this role reversal causes enormous emotional damage, for which therapy is necessary.

Denial of the need for outside help

Even when parents admit that their children have been abused, they often deny the need for outside help, insisting that their children are 'all right at home' and that they 'will soon forget about it'.

Schools and residential institutions should, whenever possible, make provision for child victims to attend therapy centres. There are many reasons why we cannot rely on parents to undertake this task.

First, it is never easy for parents to take children to treatment centres because of the painful memories and feelings of inadequacy that return whenever they undertake the journey or wait in the reception area of a centre. For parents of children with disabilities, there may be additional, guilty feelings lingering from the child's birth. Parents go through a period of grief when a child is diagnosed as having disabilities. They go through more grief when a disabled child is sexually abused. This is additional to the grief associated with the loss of a child's innocence, a break of trust and other aspects of the abuse.

To justify their broken appointments and the termination of treatment, parents are usually negative about the value of the therapy and therapists: 'It's a waste of time. The kids only draw and play. They can do that at home'.

Even when parents of disabled victims are willing to take children for therapy, some misguided professionals in schools and institutions intervene and set up barriers, denying that treatment is necessary. Influenced by the same myths as parents, teachers and social workers may also deny the damage that results from abuse when victims are disabled. Some professionals also devalue the input of other professionals, convinced that they can handle all the problems without outside help.

If children exhibit emotionally disturbed behaviours and are denied therapy by their parents, their social worker should be asked to intervene. In some circumstances, court orders may be obtained to ensure that therapy is made available.

The shortage of suitably qualified and experienced therapists

Despite the high incidence of sexual abuse involving children with disabilities, there are few therapists who have the specialist skills needed for working with victims who have major visual, hearing, speech or intellectual impairments. The

Disability and Abuse Working Party of the British Association for the Study and Prevention of Child Abuse and Neglect (BASPCAN: Kennedy, 1989) found that only 50 per cent of 'social workers' allocated to deaf people had any relevant qualifications. Some workers never actually interviewed victims with disabilities when they investigated reports; they only talked to family members and the accused, ignoring the most important people.

There is a shortage of therapists who are competent in the use of sign language for working with deaf and non verbal victims, and who understand the deaf child's view of the world. Although there were 65,000 hearing impaired children known to authorities at the time of the British research, treatment was almost non-existent. When experienced therapists were available, they were responsible for such huge populations and geographic areas that access was very limited.

Workers in this special field of child protection must have a sound understanding of child abuse and the special issues for victims with disabilities. For working with deaf and non verbal children, they must also be at an advanced level (stage 3) in signing skills. Ideally, there should be training programs that combine interviewing techniques and sign language and examine the interpreter's role in a child abuse setting.

If they have not already done so, administrators in special education and residential settings should locate therapists with expertise in working with sexual abuse victims with specific disabilities. It is best to create a support network routinely, i.e. *before* abused children have been identified.

The importance of having an independent therapist

When children undertake therapy, it is important that their teachers and parents maintain regular contact with therapists to ensure that there is continuity of treatment in the home and classroom. Teachers have prolonged contact with children and their observations can contribute substantially to the therapist's understanding of children's progress. Furthermore, they should always ask to be present at case conferences relating to children in their classes.

When no therapists are available for deaf and non verbal children, parents and teachers sometimes work together under the guidance of a non specialist counsellor. This practice should be discouraged because it fails to address the victim's need for privacy and independent, specialist help.

The presence of a teacher or parent at a therapy session could have a restricting or controlling effect. In the initial stages, the child should be free to express anger. Anger invariably focuses on parents as well as the offender. Victims need the space and permission to explore their feelings about the school. If a teacher is present, opportunities for free expression will be restricted.

Children should have a sense of control in therapy sessions. Therapy is for them. The restoration of control is necessary to compensate for the power that was removed by the abuser. Teachers and parents are probably the most powerful people in a child's life. The efforts of therapists to give victims control may be negatively influenced if either of them are present.

It takes some time for children to gain the confidence to talk about the intimate detail of what happened. It is inappropriate for them to share this detail with people who influence other aspects of their lives. Victims can express intimate details with their therapists because they know that when they leave them, they can 'switch off' until the next session. Those who see their therapists in other settings and other capacities lack that safety mechanism. They may feel a continual reminder of their abuse and will be reluctant to disclose and explore their feelings because it becomes too stressful.

Parents and siblings should have separate counselling. In cases of incest, family counselling will come much later.

INCIDENT REPORT

Class: . . . . Date: . . . .

Teacher: . . . .

Name of child: . . . .

Home address:. . . . .
. . . .

Date of birth:. . . . .

Date and time of incident:. . . . .

What was seen and by whom: . . . .
. . . .
. . . .

What was said and by whom: . . . .
. . . .
. . . .

Persons involved or said to be involved . . . .
. . . .
. . . .

Reported to: . . . .

Police:. . . . .

Child protection services: . . . .
. . . .

Other:. . . . .

Part 2

Modules

MODULE ONE

Developing Children's Self-Esteem

Aim

To develop children's confidence and self-esteem.

Note to teachers, parents and caregivers

To develop personal safety skills, teachers, parents and caregivers should use every possible opportunity to develop children's confidence and self-esteem. For optimum effectiveness, teaching strategies and activities should be integrated across the whole curriculum and used in the home. At parent workshops, participants should be invited to suggest ways in which they can increase opportunities for their children to make choices in their day to day living. Parents should also be guided on the use of positive reinforcement and positive child management strategies.

The following activities have been used effectively with non disabled children and with severely, multiply disabled children at Regency Park Centre, Adelaide, South Australia. The detail must, of course, be tailored to cater for the ability levels of each individual in the group.

Activities to develop children's self-esteem

- Ask children, in turn, to share one item of positive information about themselves, such as something that happened that made them feel really good or something that they enjoyed doing.

- Provide opportunities for children to make collages, draw or paint pictures about the things that make them feel good.

- Ask children to write, dictate or put on audiotape a letter to an imaginary friend describing themselves and aspects of their lives, such as details of what they like and dislike, how they spend their spare time, their favourite sports stars, film stars, pop stars, as well as their own physical description and family information.

- Encourage children to care for others. Provide opportunities for them to make gifts for each other and food to share. When children are absent due to illness for more than a week, encourage class members to make a giant,

'We miss you' card. Some children receive a great deal of attention but they have little opportunity to give attention to others.

- Encourage children to greet each other and say goodbye, observing mutual consideration throughout the day.

- Provide opportunities and modelling to encourage children to give positive feedback to you and to each other whenever it is appropriate.

- Make time for positive feedback sessions. Help children to pin positive, anonymous comments on the backs of those with whom they wish to communicate. Recipients read them or hear them read at the end of the session.

Care must be taken that all children receive positive feedback and good feelings do not remain the prerogative of children who already have a positive self image.

- Consider the possibility of involving children in peer tutoring and cross age tutoring. This is effectively used in school, on camps and, in South Australia, on sailing trips on the state's youth training ship. Retired members of the community could also be invited to provide a helper role for children with special needs. Help the participating guests to work out what skills they would like to share with others. Cross age tutoring needs close supervision in the early stages. When secondary school children (with and without disabilities) join an early childhood class, there is always a tendency for them to spend a substantial part of the session playing with toys, ignoring the presence of the children they are there to help. Sessions should be well planned and product based. Older children gain self-esteem because the young regard them as quasi-teachers. This gives them unaccustomed power and responsibility. They must work in partnership with teachers to foster learning using the cooperative model.

- Introduce a class newspaper which can provide opportunities for children to see their names in print. Short articles can be written about small achievements. Information about the progress of the personal safety program can be included. Children can choose the name of the paper. They make their own illustrations. Some may take photographs or, with help, conduct video interviews. The writers of the class may be appointed as reporters.

- Provide 'I'm, proud of you' and 'I'm proud of myself' boards to display children's work or information about their achievements.

- Make large class books or display boards using titles such as:

     'The nicest thing that ever happened to me';

     'The nicest thing that I ever did for someone else';

     'Things that I can do this year that I couldn't do last year'.

- Make 'Me' posters: for those with limited hand skills encourage the use of pictorial representation of the things that children like and dislike, such as colours, food and clothing.

- Use family photographs and make personal books on the lines of, 'All about ME', 'More about ME' and 'Even more about ME'.

- Use photographs and make (or buy perspex) cubes to hang or display them.

- Produce and display 'Wanted' posters with photographs and descriptions of the attractive features of children.

- Help children to draw up their own 'Bill of Rights'.

- Help children to create safety rules.

- Where possible, use or adapt the worksheets provided. Some children may be able to dictate responses. Children who cannot draw pictures should be encouraged to make collages, use personal photographs or pictures from magazines.

- Celebrate birthdays. Make large cooperative group birthday cards for class members.

- Discuss mistakes and what we learn from them.

- Let children make up plays or puppet plays and perform them for the class.

- Let children nominate a 'Person of the Week'.

- Create opportunities at the end of the day for children to discuss their successes.

- Let children give clues about someone they like; other class members have to guess who it is.

- Put a label by a mirror, 'This is the most important person in the world'.

- Help children make a 'Me Tree' showing their personal likes and dislikes on branches.

- Help children make a 'Me' collage by cutting out pictures from magazines which give a message about themselves and their likes and dislikes.

Children should be responsible for choosing and making their own illustrations. Family photographs, magazine pictures and picture postcards provide useful alternatives to drawings and collages. Ask adults to resist children's requests to draw pictures for them. If adults oblige, children become dissatisfied with their own efforts and continually seek help. Children then stop trying to do things for themselves, losing self-esteem and pleasure from creativity. When children participate in group cooperative pictures and collages, it is acceptable for adults to negotiate strategies and starting points. Adult supervisors should always acknowledge the efforts that children put into their work.

During this part of the program, teachers and parents should introduce the concept that children have rights. This is a difficult concept to teach to children who have little scope for independence. Simultaneously, it is important to teach children that, along with their rights, they also have responsibilities. They are responsible for their own behaviour and for ensuring that they do not hurt or endanger other people. These concepts require a great deal of exploration because, whilst we expect children to respect the feelings of others, it is the very fear of upsetting adults that traps victims into abusive situations.

If children are unable to complete worksheets, they should be encouraged to dictate to writers who will record their responses.

WORKSHEET

THIS IS A PICTURE OF ME

THIS IS ME

My name is _____

I live at _____

_____

_____

My telephone number is_____

My hair is _____

My eyes are _____

My face is _____

My shoes are size _____

Other features_____

_____

WORSHEET

THIS IS MY FAMILY

My parents are called: _

_ _

My brothers and sisters are called: _ _ _ _ _ _ _ _ _ _ _ _ _

_ _

I have _ _ _ _   grandmothers

I have _ _ _ _   grandfathers

My aunties and uncles are called: _ _ _ _ _ _ _ _ _ _ _ _ _ _

_ _

My cousins are called: _ _ _ _ _ _ _ _ _ _ _ _ _ _ _ _ _ _ _

_ _

I have _ _ _ _ pets. They are _ _ _ _ _ _ _ _ _ _ _ _ _ _ _ _

They are called _

_ _

THIS IS A PICTURE OF ME WITH MY FAMILY

SPECIAL INFORMATION ABOUT ME

My birthday is on _ _ _ _ _ _ _ _ _ _ _ _ and on my next birthday

I will be _ _ _ _ years old.

What I would really like for my birthday is _ _ _ _ _ _ _ _ _ _ _ _

_ _

_ _

I have fun when _

_ _

_ _

I like it when someone says _

_ _

Some people call me _

_ _

I like to be called_ _

_ _

I get into trouble when _

_ _

I wish people would _

_ _

My pet hate is _

_ _

I can be strong when _

_ _

WORKSHEET

ABOUT SCHOOL

My school is called_ _

_ _

My teacher is called _

_ _

My class is called_ _

_ _

My best friend is called _ _ _ _ _ _ _ _ _ _ _ _ _ _ _ _ _ _ _

_ _

At school I like_ _

_ _

What I hate about school is _ _ _ _ _ _ _ _ _ _ _ _ _ _ _ _ _

_ _

School would be better if _ _ _ _ _ _ _ _ _ _ _ _ _ _ _ _ _ _

_ _

But I am really good at _

_ _

I like it when someone says to me _ _ _ _ _ _ _ _ _ _ _ _ _ _

_ _

The person I would like as my school friend is _ _ _ _ _ _ _ _

_ _

THINGS THAT I AM PROUD OF...

(Examples: things that I made; things that belong to me; things I can do; something that happened at home or at school; something I did to help someone else; something I have learnt)

WHAT I LIKE ABOUT MYSELF IS

WORKSHEET

THINGS I CAN DO WELL

There are some things that I can do now that I couldn't do a year ago. These are the things I can do now:

_____

_____

_____

_____

_____

_____

_____

If I try very hard, I can _____

_____

_____

_____

_____

_____

But what I would really like to be able to do is _____

_____

_____

_____

_____

_____

_____

I LIKE...

I like it when people _

_ _

_ _

_ _

_ _

_ _

_ _

I don't like it when people_ _

_ _

_ _

_ _

_ _

_ _

And people like me when _

_ _

_ _

_ _

_ _

_ _

WORKSHEET

ABOUT HELPING

Sometimes, I like someone to help. I like to be helped when _ _ _

_____

_____

_____

_____

I don't want people to help me all the time. I don't want any help

when_ _____

_____

_____

_____

Sometimes, I help other people. I like to help other people when

_____

_____

_____

_____

This is how I help _____

_____

_____

_____

_____

WORKSHEET

BEING KIND TO EACH OTHER

Have you ever been kind to someone and they forgot to thank you?

_ _

_ _

How did you feel! _

_ _

_ _

What would you have liked to have happened?_ _ _ _ _ _ _ _ _ _

_ _

_ _

Has someone at home or school done something for you and you

forgot to thank them? _

_ _

_ _

What could you have said? _ _ _ _ _ _ _ _ _ _ _ _ _ _ _ _ _ _ _

_ _

_ _

What can you do about it now? _ _ _ _ _ _ _ _ _ _ _ _ _ _ _ _ _

_ _

_ _

WORKSHEET

AUTOBIOGRAPHICAL INFORMATION FOR 'A BOOK ABOUT ME'

- My name and address
- My age and birthday
- My class and school
- My family
- My friends
- My pets
- My favourite toys and games
- My favourite television program
- My favourite songs and singers
- My favourite film
- The person I like to play with most of all
- The person I would like to play with who doesn't play with me now
- Things I can do really well
- Things I would like to be able to do that I can't do now
- What I've learned to do this year
- The most important person in my life
- What makes me feel really good
- What makes me feel really bad
- What kind of things make me feel really happy
- What kind of things make me feel really sad
- Things that I like about other people
- Things that I don't like about other people
- Things that I'm proud of.

MODULE TWO

Developing Children's Assertiveness Skills

Aim

- To strengthen children's assertiveness skills so that they can respond to potentially unsafe situations in a convincing way.

Note to teachers, parents and caregivers

It is essential that parents and school staff are made aware of why and how children are encouraged to be assertive. Home support is crucial for enabling children to practise assertiveness outside the classroom and for learning when it is and is not appropriate to comply with the wishes of others. Some children may misuse their newly acquired assertiveness skills by refusing to accept legitimate requests, such as going to bed at a reasonable time or helping with household tasks. For that reason, we need to discuss the circumstances in which it is appropriate to refuse instructions. Children have to learn that their rights must not threaten the legitimate rights of others. This is usually incorporated in day-to-day teaching strategies and strengthened through discussion. Assertiveness requires children to use words such as, 'No' and 'Stop that' (instead of weak phrases such as, 'I'd rather not...I don't know about that...I prefer not... I don't really want to but...)

Children need to consider safe options available to them if a stronger person takes no notice and continues the unwanted behaviour. Being assertive means standing up for your own rights without stopping someone else's rights.

- Teach assertive body language, encouraging children to shake the head while saying 'No', standing (or, for wheelchair children, 'sitting up tall') and looking the person straight in the eye to say, 'No'. Adults should also help children to use their voices to shout, 'No' with real conviction.

- Teach children not to get involved in arguments. If children are asked to provide reasons, older and stronger people will use powers of persuasion which are very difficult to resist. There are times when children may need to say, 'That's not allowed' or 'My parents don't let me do that' to justify their refusal and bolster their confidence.

- Teach children that repetition is sometimes necessary. The word, 'No' may have to be repeated several times before the other person accepts the answer.

- Encourage children to use empowering language as opposed to victim language. Teach them to take responsibility for their own actions and feelings. 'He made me do it...' and 'She made me do it...' should gradually disappear from classroom vocabulary. By using such expressions, children deny responsibility for their own feelings and actions. Statements which give power to others incorporate two implicit assumptions, first, that we are not responsible and have no control over how we feel and act, and second, that our personal situation can only be bettered by others (i.e. by better luck and destiny rather than our own efforts).

- Practise using words which show that you are taking responsibility for your actions, and provide models for children. Encourage them to use replacements for the statements beginning with 'He/she made me...(angry)', He made me do it' (etc.)' with statements beginning with 'I', thereby replacing external control with an inner locus of control. For example, 'I did it because I let him upset me when he teased me', 'I did it because I was scared that...'

'I' statements are seen to be more empowering. There may be some occasions when children are bullied into things against their wishes. This can be handled by saying, 'OK, maybe he told you to do it... What could you have done instead?'

Discourage the use of other common expressions which demonstrate victim reactive attitudes. Females often use the words 'only' and 'just' to denigrate themselves. They introduce themselves on the phone with, 'It's only me'. The use of these words reveals the devaluation of self.

A lack of self-confidence is also inherent in the use of phrases such as, 'I'm trying to do...', 'I'd like to go...but...'. Compare these with direct statements of intent: I will do... I will go... I want to... I shall'.

Similarly, 'I can't do it' and 'I don't know' are often passive responses used instead of 'I don't want to do it because...'. When children claim that they have no ideas on how to resolve an everyday problem, say 'Let's pretend that you do know...what do you think you could do?' This usually brings a smile and an attempt to answer the question.

- Teach children what an emergency is and ensure that they understand that they can declare an emergency, make a fuss, scream, telephone their parents or even the police in a variety of circumstances. They need to know how to make a call, how to give their name, address, phone number, location and describe the emergency clearly and concisely. Without a child protection program, few children under the age of eight (disabled or otherwise) know their names, full addresses and telephone numbers. Accurate reporting takes a great deal of practice. Family members should be recruited in the development of these skills at home.

  Through role play (with the adult acting as the telephone operator) parents and teachers should provide opportunities for children to practise making telephone calls and reporting problems which require help.

- Teach children how to use public telephones for emergencies when they have no money or cards.

- Take children to a department store and enlist the help of the manager to demonstrate how the public address system can help lost children to find their parents. Point to public address systems at sports events, carnivals and pageants (etc.). Show children how police can use their radios to get help for lost children. Use problem solving exercises for hypothetical situations.

- Invite children to evaluate each session. Ensure that parents have opportunities to provide feedback on their problems, experiences and children's progress.

Being assertive

Sometimes it's hard to say 'No' and be assertive. It takes a lot of practice to say. 'No' with conviction. This is especially hard for females who have been taught to be submissive. Children need the chance to try their skills in 'pretend' situations. They may be able to add other suggestions from their own experiences.

Role play different situations: for example, a more powerful child says to another,

'Give me your lunch money or I'll bash you up on the way home'.

'Give me your pen (etc.)… I need it… Come on, you're not using it. I want it'.

'Let's take those glasses off that little kid just for fun'.

'I know how to get some chocolate and lollies from a shop without paying for them. You come with me and I'll show you'.

'Let's skip school today and go somewhere really good'.

Provide other situations to encourage children to think about how the victims might feel and what they can do to assert themselves.

Saying no to our friends

It is difficult to say 'No' to people we like. Children need to understand that there are times when it's all right to say 'No' and, furthermore, that other people can say, 'No' to them, without it indicating that they are no longer their friends. We all have to learn to accept 'No' without feeling angry or upset.

Opportunities should be given for children to practise saying 'No' to each other and to adults.

Saying no to bullies

Do you know what a bully is? What do bullies do? It's really hard saying 'No' to a bully, especially when the bully is bigger and stronger than you.

Take a look at the picture opposite.

Does the girl in the wheelchair want to be pushed like that? How can you tell?

Don't let bullies spoil your day.

Sometimes you can just keep out of their way. But sometimes, you might need to get help from adults to deal with bullies.

Tell me about bullying that you know of.

What can we do to stop bullies?

Remember, never bully other people.

And don't put up with bullying.

'What if...' cards

Make word cards presenting different situations for small group discussion. Ask children about their bullying experiences and make cards to suit their needs. After each situation described, insert two questions, 'How would you feel?' and 'What could you do about it?'. Refer respondents to safety issues as necessary.

BULLYING AND AGGRESSIVE BEHAVIOUR

You are playing outside when someone kicks you deliberately.

You are on a busy footpath when someone deliberately pushes you and you fall over into the gutter.

A bully pinches your arm.

You get home from school after a bad day and your mother starts shouting at you.

You are waiting in a line to go into the classroom when someone comes up and grabs you by the hair so that they can get in before you.

Bigger kids tease you and call out rude names and hassle you on the school bus.

Big boys come up to you, put their arms around you and say 'Come on...let's have a kiss'.

Story

Cindy had a new doll for her birthday. She took it to school to show it to the teacher. Her best friend wanted to play with it but Cindy didn't want to part with it. It was brand new and she was frightened that the others might break it or spoil it.

Does Cindy have to share her doll?

What can Cindy do to keep her doll safe?

Will that upset her friend?

Has something like that ever happened to you?

If Cindy says 'No' does it mean that she doesn't like her friend any more?

Do you always have to obey bigger people?

Do you always have to do what adults and bigger people tell you to do? *Discuss the following and other relevant situations.*

Suppose that an adult tells you to go outside and play with the traffic. Must you do it?

Why?

Suppose that an adult says, 'Get lost!' Must you go out and get lost?

Why?

Suppose that an adult asks you to put something in your mouth that you've never seen before. Must you do it?

Why?

Suppose that you're with a big boy in a shop. He shows you a video game and says 'I want you to steal that for me'. Must you do it?

Why?

Suppose that an adult you know says, 'Come on, give me a great big kiss'. Must you do it?

Why?

NOTE TO TEACHERS

This session may provide a suitable opportunity to introduce the very complex concept of trickery. Some children may know that their peers tease and use tricks to get their cooperation when it would not normally be given. They seldom realize that adults and older children may also use the same technique to elicit inappropriate contact.

MODULE THREE

Coping with Hazards

Aim

To improve children's general safety skills.

Note to teachers, parents and caregivers.

Parents should be encouraged to teach safety skills in the home, for example:

- how to answer the telephone safely when alone at home
- what to do if you feel unsafe when you're alone in the house
- what to do if someone comes to the door when you are in the house alone
- what to do if you hear someone breaking into your house
- what to do if a frying pan or electrical equipment, such as TV or stereo, catch fire.

Obtain leaflets and advice from organizations for the prevention of accidents. Teach safety with electricity, water, sprays, pans and kettles, medication and household chemicals, insect stings, steps and staircases and other hazards.

Introduce activities to develop safety consciousness

- Take children on a tour of buildings and outdoor areas to locate the places where they need to take special care.
- Ask children if they have seen any accidents in the school. Where did they occur? What happened? Discuss what needs to be done to avoid this happening again.
- Make a class mural showing the potentially dangerous areas. Each child contributes a different safety hazard and writes (or dictates to an adult) what that hazard is.
- Read stories about children who find themselves in situations where they need to think for themselves and act safely. Ask children how the characters would feel. Was it a happy ending or a sad ending? Why?

- Make safety awards for children who make a contribution to everyone's safety.

- Place safety captions around the room and change them regularly so that they are noticed. For example:

  'We put scissors safely in the box'.

  'We must move carefully in the wet area'.

  'We shut the cupboard door when we've finished putting things away'.

  'We must mind the steps/ramps into the classroom'.

- Encourage children to create and discuss their own safety rules.

- Conduct a search for dangerous objects: the adult should model safe handling for broken glass, plastic bags and other hazards.

- Praise children and make a record of occasions when they recognize unsafe situations and use safe practices in day-today situations.

- Discuss family rules and encourage children to decide which rules are necessary for safety at home.

- If possible, take small groups of children to visit a furnished house. With children, consider the safety features to look for in each room, for example:

  - electricity: look for loose, frayed and trailing wires, damaged points, plugs, heaters and fires near to combustible materials, water near power

  - heat: position of pans, kettles, guards to open fires

  - floor hazards: slippery floors, steps, loose mats, toys and other objects

  - poisonous and dangerous substances, especially in the kitchen, laundry cupboard and bathroom.

- Consider hazards for very young children and older people as well as hazards for those who use sticks or wheelchairs. Record findings.

- Make class books on safety in the home and safety at school.

- Discuss safety aspects of popular stories. For example, did Red Riding Hood, the Three Little Pigs, Goldilocks or the Three Bears act safely? Should Red Riding Hood walk through the forest alone and stop to talk to wolves she does not know? Goldy could have been arrested for trespassing, theft and wilful damage. The bears were very remiss in not locking their house safely and the pigs could have been injured when their houses collapsed.

- Conduct a community survey to investigate and suggest possible safety responses to community hazards, such as difficult road junctions, dangerous footpaths, dangerous playground equipment, inadequate access for wheelchairs to public services, trees obscuring traffic and traffic signs, etc. If possible, encourage children to take and develop photographs. Assist them to contact local authorities as necessary. Make a group wall story of the findings. Make a mural with captions. Produce an illustrated plan of the area highlighting unsafe places.

- Ask children to note the hazards they encounter on the way to school.

- Give children guidance on how to stay safe with people they don't know, especially people who offer lifts in cars or people who befriend them on public transport and in other places.

- Encourage the more able and older children to discuss dangers already experienced and ask,

    'What was the problem?'

    'Was it dangerous? Why?'

    'What did you do? What made it difficult?'

    'What happened? How did you feel?'

    'What do you think you should have done?'

    Dangerous experiences may include:

    - fireworks, fires or explosions

    - car accidents or near misses

    - falls from high places

    - having possessions stolen or the house burgled

    - getting lost

    - encountering thugs

    - being given a dangerous 'dare'

    - being 'tricked' into something unpleasant

    - being in the house alone when something unpleasant happens

    - wheelchairs collapsing.

- Ensure that the sensible attitudes of most children are acknowledged and praised whenever possible.

- Some children brag about their dangerous and often highly imaginative exploits. Some children are over-anxious and afraid to participate. Be sure to give these children personal attention at the end of the session and encourage discussion of reasons for their behaviour.

- Involve children in Role Play. Small groups should be asked to choose one appropriate, hazardous situation at a time. Members act out the problem and invite the audience to make suggestions for staying safe.

- Use the information for making a class book on 'Our dangerous experiences (and how we survived)'.

- If appropriate, involve parents and children in examining safety in the home from a variety of angles:

    - safety in showers and bathrooms

    - what to do in the event of a leak from a washing machine, waterbed, defective tap or hot water system

    - leaving the house unattended

    - making the house secure when indoors.

- Teach all children, whenever possible, how to use door and window locking devices.

- Give all children rules for answering home telephones. For example, children should never tell callers that they are in the house alone. It is better to teach a child to say that a parent is in the bath and will return the call if the person leaves a name and number (a bath taking much longer than a shower). Children need to know that it is acceptable to tell a lie to stay safe.

Help children to identify their unsafe feelings

It is helpful if children can learn to identify and respond to the feelings which tell them that they are not safe. Most children experience sensations in the abdomen, limbs, head and shoulders when they are startled or scared. Feelings are referred to in greater detail in Module Six.

Encourage children to work out how they can get help

This section of the program aims to make children aware that there may be occasions when they need to get help from strangers. To stay safe, the children need to be able to recognize potentially dangerous situations and work out who might be the safest person to approach for help. It is important that we do not reinforce the 'dangerous stranger' stereotype which children may have already learned from parents, peers and media.

- Children with limited mobility will have favourites among the people who handle them. Encourage them to consider why those individuals are preferred to others. Ask questions such as:

    'Suppose that you are going to a swimming pool for the first time, who would you want to be there to stop you from sinking? Why would he/she be the best person?'

    'Suppose that you were going on a picnic. Who would you like to take with you? Why would he/she be the best person? Who would you leave behind?'

- Introduce the concept of trust. Who do children trust to help them in different situations?

    How do these people make them feel? Why are they special? Who else might help?

    (Please note that 'Why' questions are difficult for children at the lower end of the developmental scale).

    Talk about why the children 'trust' the individuals they mention.

    Is it because they know, from experience, that they will help?

    Is it because they say they will help and keep their word?

    Is it because they make the children feel good inside?

    Is it because they feel safe in their hands?

- Make individual charts for children to show the names of the people who help them when they are sick, hurt, upset and the people with whom they can share happy things.

What to do in emergencies

Help children to understand emergencies. Teach them that they can declare an emergency. They can yell, shout for help, tell a helper or telephone emergency services. Teach children how to send for police, fire and ambulance. If possible, let children practise on interconnected telephones so that teachers can act as telephone operators.

WORKSHEET

CAN YOU USE A TELEPHONE IN AN EMERGENCY?

1. Lift the receiver.

2. Listen for the dial tone.

3. Dial the number you want.

4. When someone answers, tell them which service you want. The person will want to know:

   - the number of your telephone

   - who you are

   - where you live

   - where you are

   - what you want.

Use a variety of children's experiences of potentially unsafe situations for discussion.

The world of the child with disabilities is very small. Children tend to view their own experiences as the norm. Part of our responsibility as adults is to help them to realize that there are numerous possible safe solutions to different problems and they have the capacity to choose from those variations. The use of problem solving exercises is an extremely effective tool for this purpose. The adult poses a variety of different problems and asks,

'What could you do to stay safe?'

'Would that be safe? Can you think of something safe?'

'If that didn't work, what else could you do?'

'Suppose that you couldn't find a policeman, what would you do next?'

'How would you do that?'

'Suppose that there was no-one there?' etc.

Australian and New Zealand children of five to eight years demonstrated that, after exposure to a personal safety program, they could think of five to seven possible courses of action to different emergency situations, placing them in sequence: 'First, I would…and if that didn't work, I'd…'.

When appropriate, teachers should make work cards for use in small discussion groups choosing problems relevant to the children. The following have been used effectively with children in special schools and classes.

Work cards for 'Staying safe in and around the home'

What if, when you're alone in the house,

- there's a big thunderstorm, the television set suddenly goes 'bang', the picture disappears and smoke pours out of the back
- the oil in the frying pan catches fire
- you see water pouring all over the floor from the washing machine
- somebody telephones when you're alone in the house. The caller says that your mum has won a TV prize and he wants your address so that he can deliver it
- a neighbour comes round and asks you to go to his house to watch videos
- your friend calls and as he leaves, he falls and can't move. He says, 'I think I've broken my leg'
- there's a storm and the rain comes through the ceiling
- your brother/sister eats peanuts and starts to choke
- in the dark, you hear scarey noises outside your window.

Encourage the discussion of each situation. Ensure that children link the emergencies to the availability of appropriate potential helpers. Some children may suggest calling police to all situations. Check that they know how to call the appropriate service.

Staying safe in and around school

What if…

- you find that you're on the wrong bus
- you lose the others in your class when you're out on a school excursion and you have no money left
- someone you don't know sits by you on the school bus and starts teasing and upsetting you
- someone dares you to drink alcohol/smoke cigarettes or marijuana/sniff powder or adhesives/steal something from a shop. What could you do? Why? Would that be safe? What else could you do?'
- the door is locked when you get home from school and you can't find the key.

Staying safe outside the home

What if you're out by yourself and

- you get lost
- you see a gang of big boys coming towards you and you feel scared
- a big boy offers you some pills and says, 'Try some. They're great! Take these and you'll be able to do anything you want to do.'
- you want to cross a busy road.

Staying safe with strangers

What could you do to stay safe if:

- a woman you don't know says she'll give you a kitten if you go home with her
- a man says he's a policeman and wants you to help him to find a lost dog in the park
- while you're looking in a record shop, someone you don't know offers to buy you the latest hit
- an adult says, 'I'm a photographer. I'm looking for models. Would you like your photograph taken? Come with me…you'll make a lot of money'
- a lady comes up to you as you leave school and says your mum is sick and she's been taken to hospital? She says she'll take you to the hospital to see your mum
- a friend takes you to the city to do your Christmas shopping and you get lost in the crowd
- you're on the bus when a drunken man comes to sit next to you. He keeps bending over to touch you and bother you
- it's pouring with rain. A woman pulls up in her car. There are two children on the back seat. She says, 'Jump in…you're getting wet. I live just around the corner from you.'
- a man standing by a van says he's got some good video games in the back of the van. He invites you to go inside.

MODULE FOUR

It's My Body

Aim

- To develop the child's body image and body awareness.
- To introduce the concept that we own and must take responsibility for our bodies.
- To develop a positive self image by emphasizing that each child is different, has different abilities and is valuable.

Note to teachers, parents and caregivers

Ideally, sessions to develop body awareness should be accompanied or preceded by developmentally appropriate sexuality education provided by specialist teachers. In some countries, this is available through Family Planning organizations. It should be made clear to parents that children need to know about the functioning of *their own bodies*. We are not suggesting that they should be taught about adult sexuality or reproduction before they are capable of understanding it. Some children have no understanding of what their bodies are. They know that they have arms and legs and other appendages but they have no concept of the body as a whole. Children with severe disabilities are unlikely to realize that they have any responsibility for their own bodies. When asked 'Who owns your body?', they often respond, 'Mum and Dad' or provide the name of their doctor. They become so accustomed to other people handling their bodies that they have no sense of control or ownership. Most victims of abuse believe that their vulnerability was due to their lack of information. When that is the case, child victims blame their parents as much as they blame their abuser. Without protective education and regular reinforcement, most children believe that they cannot reject sexual touching by older and stronger people, not even when they recognize that it is wrong. This makes them highly vulnerable to sexual abuse (Hard, 1986; Briggs, 1991a).

The attention of parents and caregivers should be drawn to the fact that, when children are dependent on mechanical aids for mobility, those aids are part of their body image and must be treated with respect. When we touch wheelchairs, crutches or frames inappropriately and against the wishes of the owners, our actions are tantamount to emotional, if not physical abuse.

It is important to remember that children benefit from open, honest information about their bodies and their rights. Boys need to know about erections and masturbation long before they reach puberty.

Related activities

Individual children can:

- make fingerprints and handprints to demonstrate individual differences
- use large mirrors to look at and describe their bodies in a positive way (including rear and side views)
- use photographs, drawings and children's work
- create and display a personal development frieze for each group member
- draw children's silhouettes and body outlines, including wheelchairs, sticks and frames
- identify and use the correct biological names for all parts of the body
- use the worksheets in this book, with or without adult help
- make bodies from gingerbread
- use jigsaws and cut out shapes which provide opportunities to dress and undress males and females
- make a group poster, 'Nobody has a footprint (or handprint) like me'
- indicate the parts of the body which they like to be touched
- indicate the parts of the body that people may touch (if the recipient wishes to be touched).

Groups of children can

- engage in activities which draw attention to body parts such as dancing 'The Hokey Cokey', 'Hands knees and bumps-a-daisy', playing at 'Simon Says', 'Heads, shoulders, knees and toes' and 'One finger, one thumb keep moving'
- use pictorial representation, making charts, histograms, graphs to demonstrate, in different ways, how we are all different (e.g. measuring and recording height, weight, hair and eye colouring and interests)
- start 'A Book About Us' containing information about the activities and daily progress of children in the group. If children are unable to write, they should be encouraged to dictate their statements to adults who will read them back and check them for accuracy. Use class photographs for illustrations.

Our bodies are all different

We all have bodies.

I have a body.

And (name children in turn), you have a body.

Your body starts at the top of your head

And goes down to the tips of your fingers

And the end of your toes.

All our bodies are different

Where possible, encourage children to touch their bodies, first moving their hands lightly from the feet upwards towards their heads and second, from the head down to the fingers and/or toes. This can be followed up by mobile children drawing around the outlines of each others' bodies or silhouettes.

We are all different

Some of us look a little bit like our mums:

Some of us look a little bit like our dads:

Some of us even look a little bit like our brothers and sisters. But no two people are exactly the same. All our bodies are different.

Some bodies are tall
And some are short

Some people have straight hair
and some have curls

All our bodies are different!

We are all different

Some children run on their legs,
and others push past in their wheelchairs
(and even our wheelchairs are all different).

Some walk with crutches or calipers and some walk with frames.

Everyone is different.

Some walk with guide dogs.

And some walk with canes.

WORKSHEET

EVEN OUR FINGERPRINTS AND HANDPRINTS ARE DIFFERENT

This is what my fingerprints look like:

Our bodies are all different
From the tops of our heads to the tips of our toes.
Our bodies are special
And we have to take good care of them.

My Body by Peter Alsop
Chorus

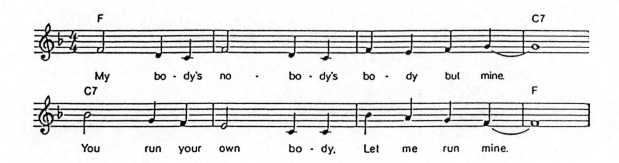

My bo-dy's no-bo-dy's bo-dy but mine.
You run your own bo-dy, Let me run mine.

(Please note that verses 1 & 4 may be inappropriate for children with physical disabilities)

1   My legs were made just to dance me around
     To walk and to run and to jump up and down.

2   My mouth was made to blow up a balloon
     I can eat, kiss and spit, I can whistle a tune.

Chorus

     My body's nobody's body but mine
     You run your own body
     Let me run mine

3   My lungs were made to hold air when I breathe.
     I am in charge of just how much I need.

4   My body loves me to peddle a bike
     Our bodies do just whatever we like.

Repeat chorus

5   Don't hit or kick me, please don't push or shove.
     Don't hug me too hard when you show me your love.

6   When I am touched then I know how I feel.
     My feelings are mine and my feelings are real.

Repeat chorus

7   Sometimes it's hard to say 'No' and be strong.
     When NO feelings come then I know something's wrong.

8   My body's mine from my head to my toe
     Please leave me alone when you hear me say, 'NO'!

Repeat chorus

9   My body's mine to be used as I choose.
     It's not to be threatened or forced or abused.

10   This is my body. It's one of a kind.
     I've got to take care of this body of mine.

Chorus

(Reproduced by kind permission of the National Film Board of Canada on behalf of the Green Thumb Theatre People; featured in the personal safety video, 'Feeling Yes, Feeling No' (Canada) and Rolf Harris' video, 'Kids Can Say No')

We are all different and special

Method

- Read or sing and discuss with children.
- Use the work sheets provided.
- Introduce related activities.
- With younger children, the beat can be emphasized with hand clapping or percussion.

> We are special people. We are all good friends.
> We are special people. We are all good friends.
> (Name child) _____ here is special,
> (Name another child) _____ is special, too.
> Of all the people in the world, there's no one just like you.
> (Repeat until every child's name has been used).

> We are special people. We are all good friends. (Repeat)
> I am very special, and you are special too.
> No one in the whole world looks just like me or you.
> _____ You are a very special person
> (refer to several or all the children in the group), 'And you
> _____ are a very special person, and you…and you…
> and you'
> We are all special people.

Activity

- Sing the song, 'My Body'
- Place a large mirror in a safe but accessible position.

  With a small group of children, ensure that each sighted child has the opportunity to appear in front of the mirror. Say:

  'Look, this is my body.

  It belongs only to me.

  I'm the boss of my body.

I tell my body what to do'.

Take children to the mirror in turn and make individual statements such as,

'Look this is _____'s body.

It's a very special body.

It can do wonderful things.

You are the boss of your body, _____

No one else's body is quite like _____'s body.

All our bodies are different.

All our bodies are special'.

WORKSHEET

WE CAN ALL DO DIFFERENT THINGS WITH OUR BODIES

We can all do different things with our bodies.

These are the things that I can do with my body without help: _ _

_____

_____

_____

_____

_____

_____

and these are the things I can do with help from other people: _ _

_____

_____

_____

_____

_____

And this is what I would like to learn to do most of all:_____

_____

_____

_____

_____

_____

You're the boss of your body

- With mobile children, find a safe space.
- Sing the Body Song.
- Remind children that they and their bodies are special.

> 'You're certainly special
> Because you're so special, how about giving yourself a big hug!
>
> There's no one quite like you...take a look around.
> No one has hair just like yours.
> No one has a face just like yours.
> You are a very, very special person.
> And your body's special too.
> Your body can do fantastic things.
> But it won't do fantastic things all by itself.
> It needs you to tell it what to do.
> It won't sit down by itself.
> It won't stand up by itself.
> You're the boss.
> You have to tell your body what to do.

Let's think of all the different things you tell your body to do.

- If children cannot provide their own suggestions, the following song might be useful.

> I can shake my body.
> I can turn it round and round.
> I can wriggle with my body.
> I can stand it on the ground.
>
> I can curl my body.
> I can roll it on the floor.
> I can lift my hand.
> And do lots more.
>
> I can turn my body round.
> And I can bend it too.
> I can move across the floor.
> What can you do?

We can all do fantastic things with our bodies.

Let's see what you can do with your body.

WORKSHEET

CHECKLIST OF THINGS THAT I CAN DO WITH MY BODY

please tick what you can do

	by yourself	with help
Get out of bed		
Get dressed		
Use the toilet		
Clean my teeth		
Bath or shower		
Wash myself		
Eat by myself		
Get on the school bus		
Get into a car		
Remember my name		
Remember my address		
Make a phone call		
Buy an ice cream		
Tell someone I need the toilet		
Choose my clothes		
Go to town on a bus		
Go shopping		
Write		
Draw		
Cook		
Change a TV programme		
Read a book		
Go to bed		
Tell people how to help me.		
And these are things I want to learn to do:		
_ _ _ _ _ _ _ _ _		
_ _ _ _ _ _ _ _ _		
_ _ _ _ _ _ _ _ _		

'I'm the boss of my body'

I have a body.
You have a body.
We all have bodies.

My body is my body.
It's nobody else's body.
My body belongs only to me.
And I'm the boss of my body.

Sometimes I like sharing my body with someone else.
Sometimes, I like to give someone a hug.
Sometimes, I like someone to hug me.

But I don't always want to be hugged.
I don't always want to be cuddled or kissed,
And if I don't want to share my body with somebody,
I can say 'No'.
It's my body and I'm the boss.
Let's all say 'No' together.

And louder! As if we really mean it!

And again!

MODULE FIVE

Some Parts of Our Bodies are Private

Aim

- To make children aware that certain parts of their bodies are 'private', namely their genitals, breasts, buttocks, anus and mouth.

- To help children to differentiate acceptable and unacceptable touching.

Please note that the mouth must be included as a 'private' body part because of the tendency of child molesters to use young children and those with disabilities (of both sexes) for oral sex.

Note to teachers, parents and caregivers

It is very important that parents and caregivers understand what is being taught in this module and why. The concept of body privacy is complex and may be alien to children who receive assistance for their most intimate hygiene. Caregivers and parents must discuss how they can help these children to increase their own contribution to self care and independence. Whenever possible, children should be allowed to choose the caregivers who undertake these personal tasks. Children recognize our hypocrisy if, while teaching them that they have the right to reject sexual misbehaviour and unwanted touching, we force them to be touched in intimate places by people they don't like.

Staff must also give consideration to the steps that will be necessary for times when children reveal that they are being touched in unacceptable ways by members of staff or voluntary helpers.

Complaints are especially troublesome in institutions where there is a shortage of care assistants or there are frequent staff changes. Children's rights and safety must always be given priority. If children indicate that they have been sexually abused, the accused person should be removed from contact with children pending formal investigations.

Make 'What if...' cards for children to discuss what someone could do if they experienced the more common forms of sexual misbehaviour, for example, if a man unzips his pants and shows you his penis.

Give guidance as necessary, such as:

Don't talk to the man.

Get away quickly.

Yell if he tries to touch you.

Tell someone you trust or if practical, send for the police.

Teachers should bear in mind that inappropriate touching can involve any part of the body.

When children become practised at problem solving, they will participate in 'What if' sessions with minimal help from teachers.

When working with non verbal students, make cue cards as a prompt for responses, either in Bliss or in English or both. When children use Bliss, make a special book with key words.

Please note that developmentally appropriate sex education is vital at this stage to ensure that children know why genitals are important and must be protected. Sex education delivered by a specialist will also ensure that children do not develop negative attitudes towards their own sexuality.

Introduce the concept of privacy

- Revise what was learned in earlier sessions.

- Start sessions with action songs or other 'warming-up' activities about our bodies.

- Proceed as slowly and as repetitiously as necessary for individual children.

- Although we aim to teach children the correct biological terms for body parts, it may also be necessary to use children's own crude expressions from time to time to ensure that they understand.

- Use diagrams of the human body (male and female) or good quality anatomically correct dolls.

- Introduce the word 'private'. What does private mean? What does it mean when you put 'private' on a door? What do children know about privacy, private places and private possessions?

- Investigate children's understanding of the word 'special'. Do children understand that when something is special, they have to take good care of it?

- To teach which body parts are 'public' and 'private', use two post boxes marked Public and Private and make cards bearing Bliss Symbols, words, or pictures of the public/private parts of the body. Children take turns in posting the cards in the right boxes.

- Teach children that 'It's OK to touch your own private parts' but only in the privacy of the bedroom or bathroom.

Parts of our bodies are private

I have a body. You have a body

We all have bodies. Our bodies are made up of lots of different parts.

Did you know that some parts of our bodies are private?

Can you remember what private means?

Private means, 'Keep out _____ don't touch _____ it's very special'.

Private means 'It's mine and I'm the boss'.

Our private body parts are so special that we keep them covered up most of the time.

We don't show them to the neighbours.

We don't show them to people in the supermarket.

We don't ask people to touch them on the bus.

We don't even share them with our friends and relatives.

Our private parts are ours.

I'm the boss of my private parts.

And you're the boss of your private parts.

They're yours and nobody else's.

Naming body parts

I have a body.

You have a body.

We all have bodies.

Our bodies have lots of different parts.

We have two eyes, two ears and a nose.

We have two legs, two feet and ten toes.

All the parts of our bodies are important.

They have important jobs to do.

Let's see if you can remember the names of the parts of your body and we'll write them down.

Use the diagrams of the male and female body on the following pages and label the main features.

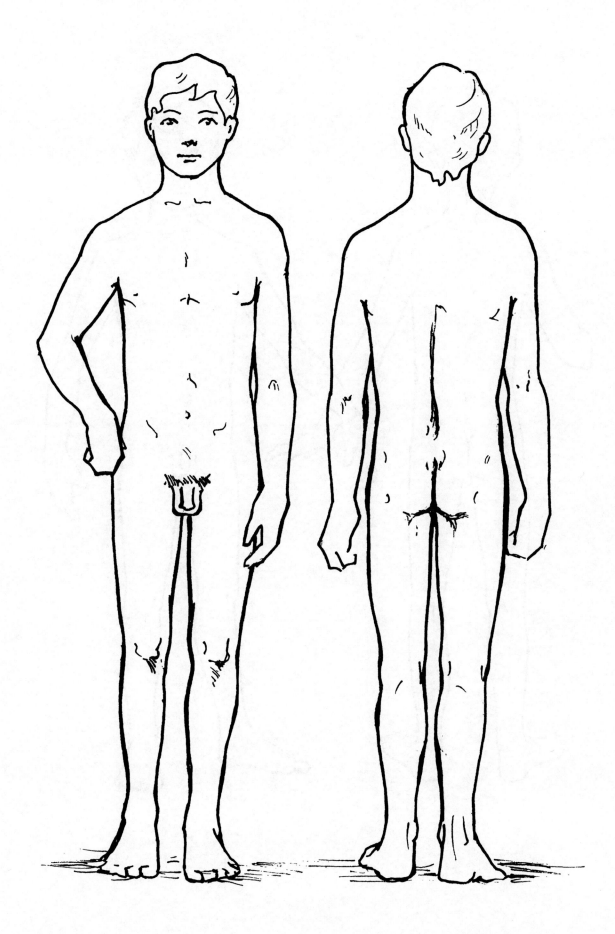

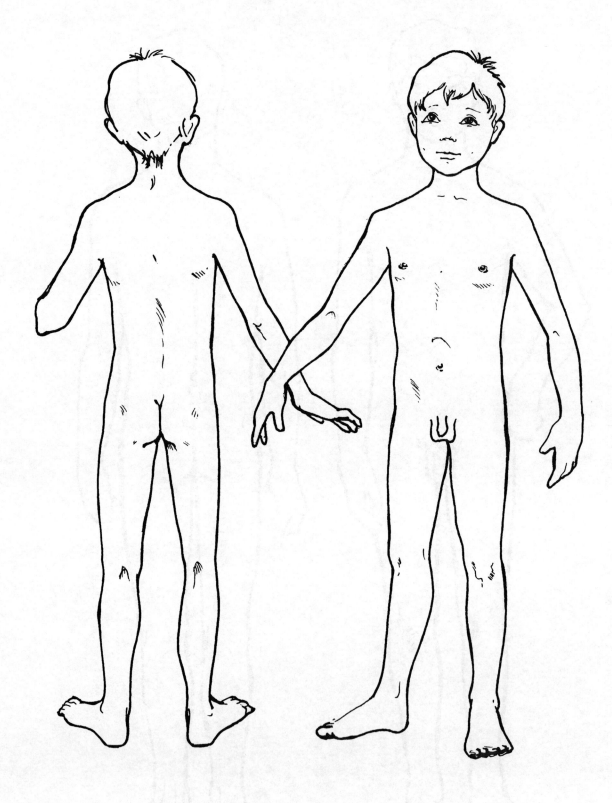

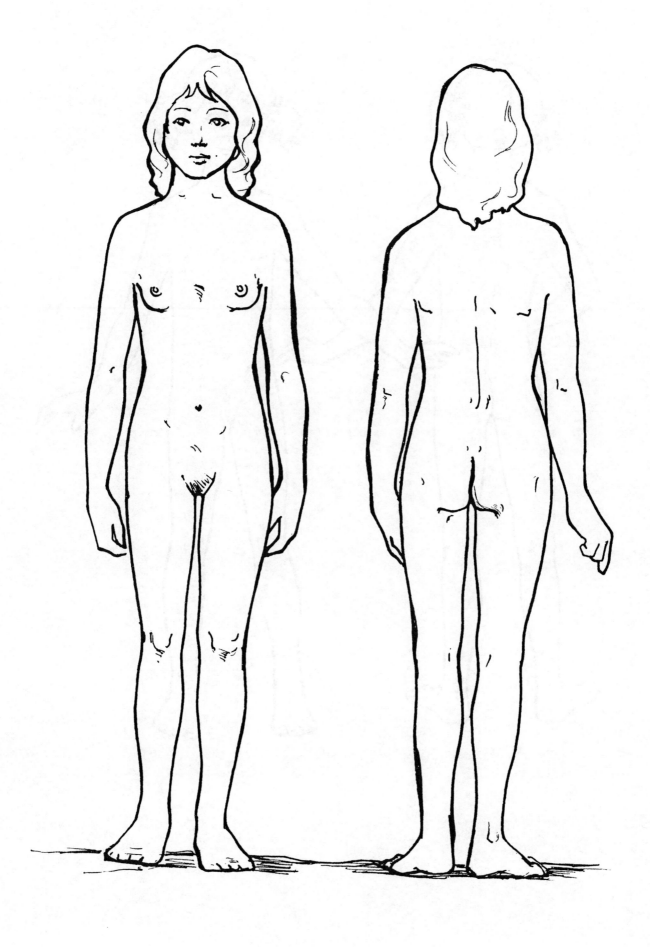

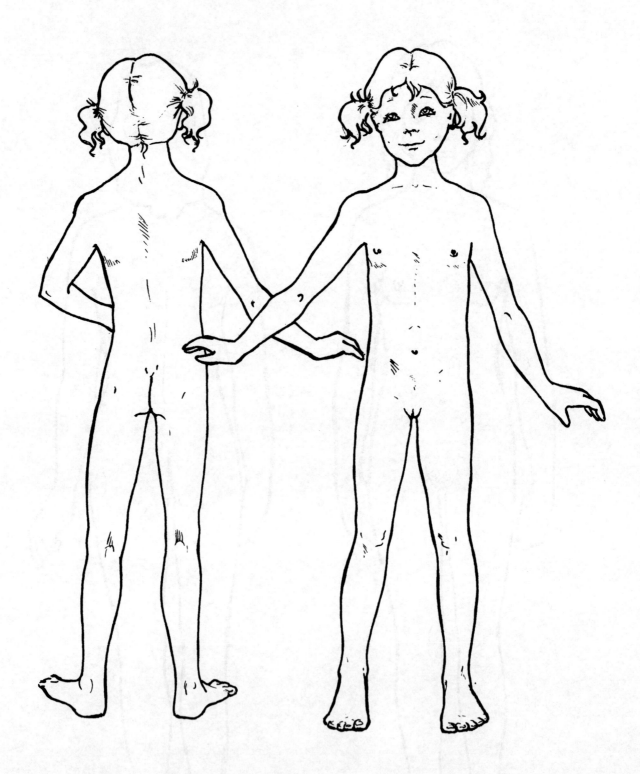

Our mouths are private places

The special, private parts of your body start at your mouth and go down to your knees. Your mouth is private. It has important work to do. Why is your mouth so important?

No one is allowed to mess around with your mouth.

No one is allowed to kiss you if you don't want to be kissed.

And, just as important, you mustn't kiss other people if they don't want to be kissed.

No one is allowed to put things in your mouth (unless you have to take doctor's medicine and can't manage to do it by yourself).

When someone tries to put something yukky in your mouth and you don't want it, say 'No!' and move away.

You are the boss of your mouth

Remember, your mouth belongs to you and no one else.

Sometimes you might like to be kissed.

But nobody wants to be kissed all the time.

Maybe you don't like the person.

Maybe you don't like the way the person kisses you.

Some people give mouth kisses that are really yukky.

Some people rub their rough chins on your face and it hurts.

Just remember, it's your body.

No one is allowed to kiss you if you don't want to be kissed.

No one is allowed to put things in your mouth.

Even if you need help to eat your food…you're the boss.

You can say, 'No!' because…

Your mouth is private.

Story: your mouth is private

(Teachers should adapt the questioning to the levels of development of individual children. The suggestions represent the maximum levels that might be expected.)

Ling was in the corner of the playground. She looked around. All the girls in her class were busy. Some were skipping. The rest were playing chasing games.

Ling can't run very fast. She wished that she could.

She was feeling a little bit sorry for herself when along came Ben. Ben is a much older boy from another class. He looked around and called out, 'Hey, Darren… Nick. Here's Ling. Come over here'.

The three boys huddled together, whispering and laughing. Ling sensed that they were laughing at her. Then, they came over.

'Ling, would you like to play with us?', Ben asked.

129

How do you think Ling felt?

Was it a good feeling or a bad one?

Ling couldn't understand why these big boys had chosen her. They could run very fast and play games that she couldn't play. But she was so pleased that they wanted to play with her that she said, 'Yes please. Which game are you playing?'

'It's a new game', said Ben. 'You've never played it before'.

Darren and Nick both giggled. Ben told them to shut up.

Darren and Nick turned away to try to stop laughing.

Ling felt a little bit uncomfortable and a little bit worried. She didn't know why she felt like that. She was so pleased that the big boys wanted to play with her that she didn't take any notice of her feelings.

'The first thing you have to do is to close your eyes', said Ben 'And then you open your mouth very wide. You keep it open until I tell you to close it. And then you get a special surprise. Promise you'll do that?'

'I promise', said Ling.

She closed her eyes. She opened her mouth. But now she was feeling very uncomfortable indeed. Her heart was beating faster and she held her breath. Do you know why she felt worried? Ben came closer to Ling. She heard the other two boys squealing with laughter. She now had such a bad feeling that she opened one eye and peeped just a teeny weeny bit. Her mouth was still wide open. Out of the corner of her eye, Ling saw that Ben was just about to put a big, fat, slippery, wriggling garden worm into her mouth.

How do you think she felt?

Was it a good feeling or a bad one? Why?

Which parts of her body told her that she was having a bad feeling?

If someone was putting something nasty in your mouth, it would give you a yukky, bad feeling too. Which parts of your body tell you that it's bad? Where do you get those funny feelings that make you feel uncomfortable?

What should Ling do?

Who should she tell?

What should she say?

Why do you think those boys played that nasty trick on Ling?

Just remember that your mouth is private. That means, 'Keep out'. You can put good food in your mouth. You can put your toothbrush and toothpaste in your mouth. You can put medicine in your mouth if it comes from the doctor. Your dentist can look in your mouth, too. But other people must keep out. Private means, 'Keep Out'. Don't let anyone put anything in your mouth. Take good care of your mouth; it is an important part of your body.

We have other private places

You know that your mouth is private.

Did you know that breasts are private too? Some people call them boobs or tits, but today we're going to use the adult words.

Everybody has breasts.

When girls grow up, their breasts change shape ready for feeding babies. When boys grow up, their breasts don't change. Let's label the breasts of the boy and girl in the pictures.

Breasts are a private part of your body.

Nobody is allowed to play with your breasts.

Nobody is allowed to touch them if you don't want to be touched.

Breasts are private places – they're yours and you're the boss.

If you're not feeling well, the doctor might need to listen to your chest with a stethoscope but, if you're a girl, a nurse or a parent or a member of the school staff should be there with you. Those are the rules.

And more private places

Our other special and private parts are tucked away out of sight between our legs. We cover them up with our pants.

Do you know what they are called?

A boy has a penis and testicles between his legs. They are very special and private things to have if you are a boy.

Girls have a vulva between their legs. The vulva is a bit like the top of a box of tissues. It protects what's inside and keeps it clean and safe. Inside the vulva is an opening called the vagina. Vulvas and vaginas are very special and private things to have when you are a girl.

Remember, private means that those parts of your body belong to you. You're the boss of your special, private places.

NOTE TO TEACHERS, PARENTS AND CAREGIVERS

It is likely that some girls with serious disabilities have never seen their own genitals. In sexuality education, it is customary for educators to assist them to look at the construction of their bodies in privacy by providing them with mirrors and diagrams. Sexuality education should also inform children why their genitals are important, what purpose they serve and why we must take good care of them. It is important that educators transmit a 'sex-positive' message, acknowledging that sexual touching is pleasurable. In general, it is customary to tell children that our genitals are special and private places because we will want to share them with a special partner when we grow up. Teachers are urged to utilize the services of specialists for this difficult and important task.

Other private places

We have some more private places. These are the places we cover up with our pants.

We all have buttocks.

We all have an anus.

Some children call it their bum or their bottom but we're using grown-up names today.

Your buttocks and your anus are private, special places.

Your anus is very important.

It's the opening that gets rid of the faeces (waste food/rubbish/shit) when you go to the toilet.

You have to look after that part of your body and keep it clean.

We don't play around with it.

We don't let anyone else play around with it.

And we never put things inside it.

We dry it well when we have a shower or a bath.

And if we don't look after our anus we're likely to get sore.

And that's very, very uncomfortable.

It someone wants to play around with your private parts, you can say 'No!' Tell them to go away, and tell someone about it.

Remember, your body is yours.

You're the boss of your body.

All of your body is special and you have to look after it.

But the parts of your body from your mouth to your knees are extra special and private.

Private means that no one can touch them without your permission. Private means they're yours.

Private means, you're the boss.

These are the rules for your private places

If doctors or nurses need to touch the private parts of your body, your mother or a nurse or a member of the school staff will be there with you.

If you need help to go to the toilet, the people who help you must keep to the rules.

If they have to touch your private places…these are the rules:

> No one is allowed to play around with your private places
>
> No one is allowed to tickle you in your private places
>
> No one is allowed to look at your private places just for fun
>
> And we don't show our private places to other people

Your private places are yours

They're no one else's

You're the boss

Private means 'Keep out!'

If someone breaks the rules and touches your private places just for fun, you can do something about it because you're the boss. What do you think you can do?

You can say 'no'

You can say 'No' to bigger people who want to touch your body just for fun.

You can say 'No' to grown-ups who want to touch your body just for fun.

You can say 'No' to other kids if they break the rules and touch your body, your sticks, your frame or your wheelchair when you don't want to be touched. Say 'NO', get away and tell someone about it. Who could you tell?

Say 'no' and tell someone

If someone tries to lift up
your dress, say 'No! Stop that!
It's not allowed'

If someone puts their hands in your pants say 'No' that's not allowed. People aren't allowed to do that to kids'.

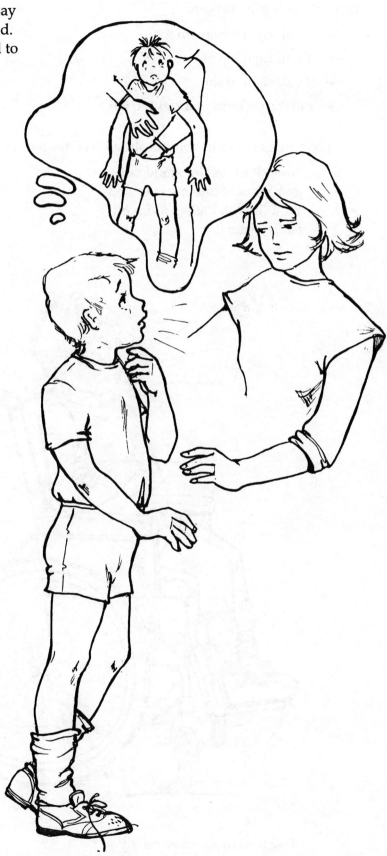

Remember, it's your body. You're the boss. You could say 'No' and tell somebody... Who could you tell?

Shout 'no'

If someone touches or tickles the private parts of your body, or if someone asks you to touch their private parts:

- it's all right to scream
- it's all right to yell
- it's all right to shout
- and it's definitely all right to tell.

Let's hear how loud you can shout 'No!' Stop it! That's wrong!'.

Now sit up tall (or stand tall),
look straight into my eyes and
shout it even louder, as if you
really mean it.

Now turn to someone near you
Sit up/stand tall. Move back a little
and look them straight in the eye.

Problem to solve: rejecting sloppy kisses

Tara has a nice aunty who takes her out in her wheelchair. Aunty has a big car and the wheelchair fits in the back. Tara's aunty is kind. She buys ice creams and treats and takes Tara to 'Wheelchair sports'.

The problem is this: Tara's aunty is forever kissing people. She kisses Tara's mum and Tara's dad and anyone else who happens to be around.

Tara hates being kissed. Her aunty gives those wet, sloppy kisses right on her mouth. They're not just wet and sloppy, they go on and on. Tara hates it so much that, when her aunty rings to invite her out, she pretends to be too sick or too tired to go. That's a pity because she likes wheelchair sports (as well as ice creams and treats).

'What's wrong with you?', mum asked crossly when Tara said that she didn't want to go out with her aunty. 'You know she likes going out with you. She'll be really upset'.

'But I don't like the way she kisses me', said Tara at last.

'Don't be silly', mum said. 'She loves you. That's why she kisses you. She'll be upset if you tell her you don't like being kissed. You'll just have to put up with it. We all have to put up with things that we don't like'.

Is Tara's mum right?

Does Tara have to put up with being kissed when she doesn't want to be kissed? Why?

Tara doesn't want to upset her aunty. How can she stop the kisses without upsetting aunty's feelings? What can Tara do?

What can she say?

NOTE TO TEACHERS

If children cannot think of solutions for themselves, ask closed questions such as 'Could she tell aunty that...?'. Follow these with, 'What else could she do?'

Make 'What if...' cards for group discussion using puppets

The puppet says: 'Hello, my name is _____ and

- When I was coming to school this morning, a man unzipped his pants and showed me his penis.
- I was playing with some kids and some big boys said they'd pay me to take all my clothes off.

Ask the group:

'How would _____ (the puppet) feel when this happened?'

'What could _____ (the puppet) do to stay safe?'

'What if this person tried to grab him/her?'

'What should _____ (the puppet) do later?'

MODULE SIX

Learning About Our Feelings

Aim

This module aims to help children to:

- become more aware of their different feelings
- find acceptable ways of expressing their feelings
- identify and respond appropriately to feelings that are worrying, yukky, confusing, frightening or uncomfortable
- realize that when we feel worried, confused or scared, we can do something about it.

Note to teachers, parents and caregivers

Children are great protectors of adults. They sense our needs and feelings and will disregard their own to please us. This makes them very vulnerable to exploitation.

Children are taught early in life that being 'good' means being obedient to adults. Simultaneously, they learn that their own feelings are irrelevant. Children who have not undertaken a personal safety program agree that 'Kids have to do what adults tell them', even if the adult's behaviour is 'rude', bad or wrong' (Briggs, 1991a, 1991b).

When parents, teachers and caregivers are not aware of the importance of children's feelings, they often discourage children from expressing them. It is often assumed, wrongly, that children with serious disabilities do not experience the same kind of feelings as other people.

Child sexual abuse by known and trusted adults can be confusing to victims because it is usually preceded by affectionate and seductive behaviour which produces good feelings. For children who lack physical affection at home, sexual fondling can be gentle and pleasant, exciting or comforting and, simultaneously, yukky and worrying. At the same time, adult sexuality can shock and the demand for secrecy bewilders children.

For personal safety, it is helpful if children can recognize and respond to worrying and confusing feelings to make themselves safe. This cannot be taught in a few sessions: children need practice in the expression of feelings in their day-to-day lives. They need to know that feelings can change and when good feelings are replaced by worrying ones, they should respond to those worrying feelings. They need reassurance that their acceptance of one form of behaviour does not commit them to continuation, least of all if the behaviour changes. We are allowed to change our minds and say, 'No'.

'Feeling' is a very difficult concept for non verbal children. It may be necessary to teach it using its 'mirror image' concept, thought. Use cue cards, 'I think' and 'I feel'.

Passive children seldom realize that they can do anything to make things better. When young children talk about their 'scared feelings', they usually refer to fears of the dark and being alone in the house. They are afraid of weird shadows on bedroom walls and strange noises in the night (which are attributed to monsters, ghosts, robbers and violent strangers).

When there is no parental or school encouragement for children to communicate their feelings, they usually keep their fears to themselves. They do not realize that, if responsible adults know that they are afraid of the dark, they will provide a torch or a low-watt, shadow free night light. Unless they have participated in a personal safety program, children do not know that their parents will replace babysitters who misbehave.

Teachers, caregivers and parents need to consider what they will do if they receive important information from children which involves the home or school. If children have already attempted to communicate (non reportable) problems and anxieties to parents without success, it may be necessary for teachers to seek children's permission to intervene.

If children's revelations suggest the need for changes to school routines, it may be necessary for parents and staff to discuss the problems with administrators.

Most children trust adults implicitly because they have only been taught to fear the ubiquitous male monster–stranger.

When asked about their fears, young children may only refer to imaginary beings and it is usually necessary to ask specific questions such as, 'What do people do to make you feel scared?'

Some children will say that they are afraid of people who dress up as monsters and ghosts and wear masks which disguise their identities. Most young children will refer to fears of Halloween festivities and violent television.

Many children say that they are afraid of adult and peergroup violence. Some children may tell you that they become involved in parents' fights. Other may have already formulated simple strategies for avoiding domestic violence.

Draw children's attention to the warning signs and body changes that occur when we experience worrying feelings. These body changes alert us to the fact that we are no longer safe.

Some teachers heighten children's awareness by blowing up a very large balloon and, without knotting it, they carry it around the room. Some children cringe momentarily, fearing that the balloon may burst or fly towards them. When children react in this way, the teacher immediately asks them to describe how their bodies felt when they thought that the balloon might explode or be released. Which of their body parts felt different? Were those new feelings good or bad feelings? What did the children want to do to make themselves feel safe?

Needless to say, this activity should NOT be used with very nervous children or those with heart defects. There are, of course, ethical considerations relating to modelling. Can we justify giving children 'bad' feelings, albeit momentarily, for educational purposes when we are aiming to teach them neither to give nor receive bad feelings?

If there is a sudden, loud noise, such as the banging of a door, use the opportunity to encourage children to describe their feelings.

To emphasize these body changes, draw the outline of a child and assist group members to arrow the locations of their 'scared' or anxious feelings with labels such as,

'Mandy says that when she's scared, she gets a funny feeling in her throat'.

'Jason gets a tingling feeling in his shoulders'.

Make and use a 'feeling box'

Depending on the developmental levels of the children, it is recommended that teachers introduce different fabrics and textures to demonstrate the notion that some touching feels better than others and some touching gives 'yukky' feelings.

A 'Feeling Box' can be made from an old carton. For sighted children, make a hole in the top that is only just large enough for a hand to pass through it. Ensure that there are no gaps in the sides of the box. To prevent children from seeing the contents, attach an old, toeless sock to the hole. Participants then have to put their hand through the sock to reach the objects.

Materials of different, contrasting textures should be provided. These may include hessian, coarse sandpaper, domestic steel wool, pan scourers, satin, silk, velvet and ice.

Children are asked to describe the first article that they touch. Does it give a good or a bad feeling? Why does it feel good or bad? ('Why' questions are often difficult to answer). What does it feel like? Is it a good touch, a worrying touch or a yukky touch that they want to stop?

Some teachers use 'yukky' substances such as manufactured 'slime', dough, plasticene, offal, an uncooked (whole) fish, pretend spiders or obnoxious substances that can be found in novelty shops. These are very effective in producing 'yukky' responses. There are ethical issues to consider however: we are about to teach children that they should neither give nor receive yukky or bad touches and it is important that we model what we teach.

Children are asked to describe how they feel before they put their hands in the box. They are asked to describe their feelings again when they touch an object and, once more, when they remove it. Do their feelings change when they remove the objects and see them? Do they get a good feeling or a yukky feeling? If it is a yukky feeling, which parts of the body tell them that they feel yukky? What does 'yukky' feel like?

What do they want to do when they get a yukky feeling?

When pretend insects are used and children respond negatively to what is in their hands, they should be invited to describe how they felt when they thought that they had picked up a real spider, etc. Did their feelings change when they realized that the spider was not real? Which parts of the body told them that they did not like what they were holding?

A further extension of this exercise would be to provide different, safe odours using herbs, perfumes, flowers, disinfectant, foods and spices for children to assess and chart for good and bad feelings. A group book can be made to include, 'Smells that give us good and bad feelings'.

Blindfolds are often used for school activities relating to the senses. However, it is NOT recommended that teachers use blindfolds for children with disabilities because they often panic when they lose their sense of control.

Suggestions for puppet or role plays

- The larger puppet threatens the smaller one that he will give him a beating on the way home from school.

  Ask children how the small puppet might feel.

  What can he or she do to stay safe?

- It is time for lunch. One puppet goes to his bag and finds that his lunch has been stolen.

  How does he feel?

  What can he do about it?

- A puppet confesses to the class that his parents left him with a babysitter last night and the babysitter showed him some 'rude photographs'. The puppet tells the audience how he felt and asks what he can do to make sure that it doesn't happen again?

  Give each child an opportunity to make a suggestion

- A puppet says that he is lost in a big, busy department store at Christmas. The puppet looks around for mummy puppet but can't find her. The audience is asked how the puppet might feel. What should he do to stay safe?

- A puppet has accidentally spilt a drink. Daddy puppet is very cross and shouts and pushes, calling her bad names. Ask children

  'How does the small puppet feel?'

  'What could he do about it?'

Encourage the appropriate expression of feelings

Encourage children to express their feelings when opportunities arise. When children resort to aggressive behaviour, it is usually because they lack the knowledge and skill to achieve their needs by acceptable means. When a dispute occurs, stop the action and tell all participants that they will be heard.

Encourage each child, in turn, to explain what happened in terms of their own feelings. For example:

'I was upset because my pencil wasn't there when I needed it;
I was angry because he took my pencil without asking me and I was scared that I wouldn't get it back'.

Each child involved in the dispute is asked how he or she would like the situation to be handled 'next time', for example:

'I'd like him to ask me for it nicely'.

The teacher asks primary aggressors if they are aware of the relevant rules of behaviour. What were their needs? How could they have met their needs in more appropriate ways?

Victims are invited to comment on these suggestions. How do they feel about them? Can they suggest better methods?

Ideally, the teacher gains a consensus and participants are asked to verbalize the agreement they have reached.

In the early stages, the process is slow. However, once the procedure is learned, children will resolve situations for themselves without adult intervention. This develops self discipline and reduces opportunities for friction.

Brainstorm 'what we can do when we get bad feelings'

- Discuss what kind of things make us feel: sad, worried, angry, upset, stupid, lonely, scared, sick, fed up, useless, guilty, envious, frustrated, disappointed etc.
- Enquire what children can do to stop the bad feelings.
- Discuss ways of handling the problems.

We all have feelings

Everybody has feelings.
I have feelings, you have feelings.
We all have feelings.
Sometimes they are good feelings
And we want them to last for ever.
Sometimes, they are bad feelings
And we want them to stop.

How are you feeling today?

Look at the faces opposite and point to the one that feels like you.

Good feelings

Sometimes we feel happy.
And sometimes we feel sad.
And sometimes we feel neither happy nor sad.
Happy feelings are the good ones that we like to keep.
We want them to last for ever and ever.
Tell me about some of the happy feelings that you like…the feelings that you want to last for ever and ever and never stop.

The teacher should use brainstorming methods to create a group list of 'Good feelings that we like'.

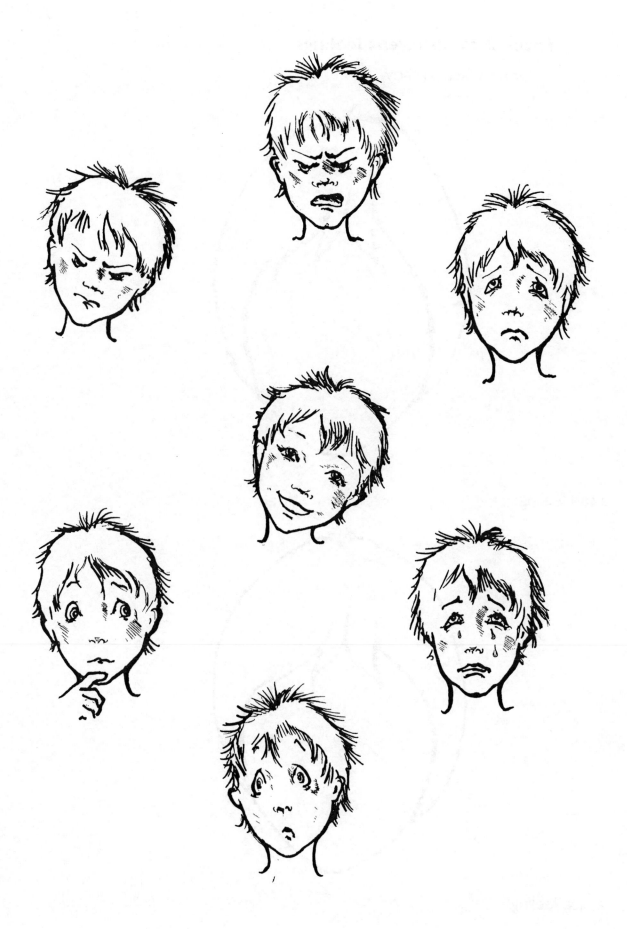

WORKSHEET

Faces show different feelings

Draw a face to show:

a sad feeling

a nice feeling

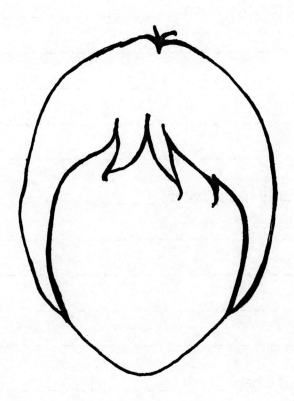

a confusing feeling

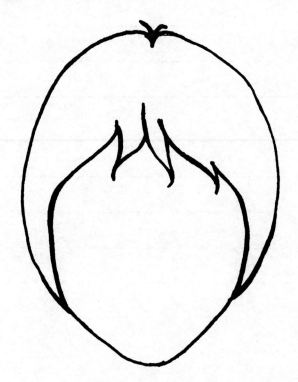

a yukky feeling

MY GOOD FEELINGS

I have good feelings when: _

_ _

_ _

_ _

_ _

And I feel really happy when: _ _ _ _ _ _ _ _ _ _ _ _ _ _ _ _ _ _

_ _

_ _

_ _

I feel pleased when: _

_ _

_ _

_ _

I like it when: _

_ _

_ _

_ _

_ _

WORKSHEET

EVERYTHING THAT WE HEAR GIVES US FEELINGS

Everything that we hear gives us feelings.
Sometimes, we don't like what we hear.
We get bad feelings and want them to stop
Sometimes we love what we hear.
We get good feelings and want to hear more

These are the things I like to hear: _ _ _ _ _ _ _ _ _ _ _ _ _ _ _ _

_ _

_ _

_ _

_ _

_ _

_ _

_ _

And these are the things I don't like to hear: _ _ _ _ _ _ _ _ _ _

_ _

_ _

_ _

_ _

_ _

_ _

_ _

Everything that we taste gives us feelings

Our bodies give us lots of different feelings.

Some are good feelings that we like.
Some are bad feelings that we want to stop.

Everything that we taste gives us feelings.
Everything that we lick or swallow or put inside our mouths gives us feelings.

When we get good feelings, we say, 'That was yummy. Can I have some more?'

When we get bad feelings, we say, 'Yuk! That tastes awful'.

What do you like to taste?

What do you hate to taste?

Make lists of tastes that give good feelings and tastes that give bad feelings.

NOTE TO TEACHERS

A similar routine should be adopted to draw children's attention to their feelings relating to their sense of smell and feelings associated with sight.

Sad feelings

Sometimes, we get sad feelings.

Tell me, what makes you feel sad?

What do you do when you feel sad?

It helps to share your troubles with someone.
If you're feeling sad, tell someone about it.

Who could you tell?

Tell someone who will listen and help.
Sad feelings go away when we share them with somebody.

What is happening in this picture

What is happening in the picture opposite?

Where do you think these boys and girls are?

That's Kim standing by the door. How do you think she feels?

How do you think the other people are feeling?

What do you think they're talking about?

Have you ever felt left out of a group like that?

What happened?

What did you do?

What other unhappy feelings have you had?

Sometimes we get yukky feelings

Sometimes we get yukky feelings
Yukky feelings are bad feelings.
They make you feel a bit sick inside.
Yukky feelings make you say, 'Ugh! Yuk! Stop it!'.
What gives you yukky feelings?

Remember, you're the boss of your body.

If someone does something that gives you a 'yukky' feeling, tell them to stop it.

People aren't allowed to do yukky things to kids.

Sometimes, people make us feel scared

Sometimes, people do things that make us feel scared.

What sort of things make you feel scared?

What can you do to make yourself safe when you get those scared feelings?

DEEP END
5' 6"

When you feel scared, tell someone about it. Tell someone who will listen and help you.

Who can you tell?

WORKSHEET

You are walking down a corridor when, all of a sudden, you see a wheelchair coming towards you at a very fast speed. There's no room for you to get out of the way.

Which parts of your body tell you that you're not safe?

My head feels _

My tummy feels _

My legs go _

My knees _

My hands _

My neck _

My hair _

and_ _

_ _

_ _

_ _

What are those messages telling you to do? _ _ _ _ _ _ _ _ _ _ _ _

_ _

_ _

_ _

_ _

_ _

WORKSHEET

THESE ARE THE THINGS THAT MAKE ME FEEL SCARED

Sometimes, people do things that make us feel scared. It's all right to feel scared. Everyone feels scared some time.

I get scared when: _

_ _

_ _

_ _

I get scared when other kids: _ _ _ _ _ _ _ _ _ _ _ _ _ _ _ _ _ _ _

_ _

_ _

_ _

I get scared when grown-ups: _

_ _

_ _

_ _

And I know kids who are scared of: _ _ _ _ _ _ _ _ _ _ _ _ _ _ _ _ _

_ _

_ _

_ _

And this is what we can do to stop those scared feelings: _ _ _ _

_ _

_ _

_ _

TELL SOMEONE ABOUT IT!

IF...

If I feel scared in the dark, this is what I can do to make the scary feelings go away:

_____

_____

If I feel scared when I'm in the house by myself, this is what I can do to make myself feel better: _____

_____

_____

If I'm feeling scared in a thunderstorm, this is what I can do to make myself feel safe:

_____

_____

If I feel scared of a grown-up, this is what I can do to make the scary feelings go away:

_____

_____

If I feel scared while watching television, this is what I can do to make myself feel better: _____

_____

_____

We all get scary feelings but we do something to make them go away: _____

_____

_____

WORKSHEET

Just suppose that you are crossing the road when, all of a sudden, a car comes around a corner at a very fast speed. The car is coming straight towards you.

How do you feel? (Circle the feelings)

Safe   Unsafe   Frightened   Surprised   Happy

Shocked   Sad   Strong   Worried   Brave

Good   Bad   Scared   and:

Just suppose that you open a cupboard door and a mouse runs out and runs over your feet.

How do you feel?

Good   Bad   Startled   Shocked   Yukky

Worried   Pleased   Surprised   Safe   Unsafe

Scared   Happy   and:

- -

- -

- -

- -

- -

- -

- -

- -

- -

EVERYBODY FEELS ANGRY AT SOME TIME

Everybody feels angry at some time.
It's all right to feel angry.
But you must tell someone about it.
It's best that we share your angry feelings
Not keep them to ourselves.

This is what we look like when we're angry:

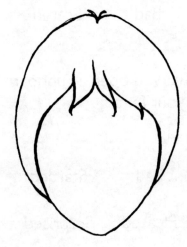

This is what makes me angry: _ _ _ _ _ _ _ _ _ _ _ _ _ _ _ _ _ _ _

_ _

_ _

_ _

_ _

_ _

And this is what I can do when I'm angry:_ _ _ _ _ _ _ _ _ _ _ _ _

_ _

_ _

_ _

_ _

156

Worrying (or confusing) feelings

NOTE TO TEACHERS, PARENTS AND CAREGIVERS

The concept of worrying (or confusing) feelings is extremely difficult for children at the lower end of the developmental scale to grasp. It is helpful if children recognize these feelings because, when sexual behaviour is introduced by adults, the experience is often marked by feelings of confusion. Whilst children's instincts may tell them that what is happening is wrong, offenders assure them that 'everything is all right'. Sexual touching may even feel 'all right'. Confusion places children in a weak position and makes them more vulnerable to exploitation.

Discuss with children

Sometimes, our feelings are worrying (confusing), We aren't really sure whether we like them or not.
We get a very funny tummy feeling that we don't like.
That funny feeling tells us that something's wrong.
It tells us to get away and stay safe.
When do you get those funny, worrying feelings?

Sometimes, we like the person we're with but we don't like what that person is doing. Has that ever happened to you? Tell me about it.

Good feelings can change to worrying ones

NOTE TO TEACHERS

To stay safe, children need to know that the acceptance of someone's behaviour in the first instance is not binding: we can change our minds at any time, especially if the circumstances change. This is hard for young children and those with developmental disabilities to understand.

Teachers can help by giving children opportunities to practise the use of eye-to-eye contact and assertiveness skills. Teachers should also create opportunities for children to practice saying, 'No' in a convincing way.

Sometimes, we feel good and we don't want those good feelings to stop.
It can be fun to wrestle with other kids.
It can be fun to wrestle with someone we like.
But we don't want to wrestle all the time.

Sometimes, wrestling goes on for too long.
Sometimes, it gets rough.
And we want it to stop.
When we want something to stop, what should we say?
What should we do?

Suppose that you're wrestling with your friends.

The wrestling goes on too long – it hurts, and they won't stop.

What can you do?

WORKSHEET

SOMEONE MIGHT ASK US TO DO THINGS THAT DON'T FEEL RIGHT

Sometimes, when people ask us to do things, we get a funny, worried feeling. It doesn't feel right.

If someone asks me to do something that doesn't feel right, this is what I can say:

_____

_____

_____

_____

_____

This is what I can do: _____

_____

_____

_____

_____

And these are the people I can tell: _____

_____

_____

_____

_____

_____

If you have worrying (or confusing) feelings, you can say,
'Please don't do that. I don't like it'.
What else can you say?

And if people don't take any notice when you say, 'No',
Tell someone about it.
Tell someone who will help you.
Who can you tell?

Draw a picture of yourself without any worries.

This boy feels worried because he is alone in the house

That's a pity because it can be fun being in the house by yourself.

What can this boy do to make himself feel safer?

This boy feels scared when he sees shadows on his bedroom wall

What could he do to make himself feel safer in his bedroom at night?

WORKSHEET

MOST TIMES I FEEL SAFE AND HAPPY

I feel safe and happy when I'm _____

_____

_____

_____

_____

I feel very safe when I'm with _____

_____

_____

_____

I don't feel safe when _____

_____

_____

_____

And I don't feel safe with _____

_____

_____

_____

_____

WORKSHEET

MY BAD FEELINGS

I feel angry when: _

_ _

_ _

I feel upset when: _

_ _

_ _

I feel uncomfortable when: _ _ _ _ _ _ _ _ _ _ _ _ _ _ _ _ _ _

_ _

_ _

I feel a little bit scared when _ _ _ _ _ _ _ _ _ _ _ _ _ _ _ _ _

_ _

_ _

I sometimes feel confused when: _ _ _ _ _ _ _ _ _ _ _ _ _ _ _ _

_ _

_ _

And I get yukky feelings when: _ _ _ _ _ _ _ _ _ _ _ _ _ _ _ _

_ _

_ _

When you get bad feelings, don't keep them to yourself.
Tell someone.
Tell a friend.
Tell your mother or a teacher.
Bad feelings get better when you share them with someone.

Keep on Telling until Someone Does Something to Make You Safe

Talking About Touching

Before using this Module, please revise previous work.

Aim

- To reinforce and extend the concepts taught in Modules 2–5.
- To provide opportunities for children to practise saying 'No' to unwanted or inappropriate touching.
- To teach children that they can tell a responsible adult if
    - someone touches them sexually
    - they are confused about the appropriateness of touching
    - their requests to desist are ignored by the toucher.
- To teach children safety rules for touching and identify people who will help.

Notes for teachers, parents and caregivers

When we deny that children are sexual beings, we deny that they enjoy touching themselves and each other. Touching is an essential part of life. It also becomes an issue for children with disabilities. This can be seen in the table opposite:

Teachers and parents should take note of the fact that the differentiation of acceptable and unacceptable touching behaviour is often the most difficult skill to teach. It must be tackled concisely and conscientiously because it is the central goal of all education for child protection. There is often a vast difference between what parents and teachers think they said and what children heard and understood. Messages must be clear and unambiguous. Children cannot take vague hints about touches or feelings and transfer them to sexual experiences with those on whom they are emotionally or physically dependent.

If children cannot make the critical distinction between appropriate and inappropriate behaviour, their safety is jeopardized. In other words, without clear information that adults and older kids are never allowed to play or mess around with children's genitals for fun (and vice versa), the message will not be meaningful.

Positive aspects of touching Touching is needed for:	Issues relating to touching affecting children with disabilities
Basic care	Overly protective care
Communication	Child's right to say 'No' to unwanted touching
Fun and games	Child's right to personal space
Pleasure	Denial of sexuality
Love	Negative communication
Comfort	Punishment
Reassurance	Cultural differences
Positive reinforcement	Sexual touching between peers
Acceptance	Touching used to gain power and control
Bonding	Sexual abuse
Security	Touched by dozens of people
Praise	regardless of wishes
Therapeutic care	Invasive touching
Social greetings	Painful & uncomfortable touching
Friendship	Over familiarity and intimate touching
Acknowledgement	
Body awareness	Teasing
Approval	Medical touching
Support	Physiotherapy/massage
Mutual sexual relationships	Self-touching at inappropriate times

In deference to taboos and the feelings of parents and teachers, many program designers have done everything possible to avoid transmitting that simple message to children. They hoped that by teaching children to escape when they experience unsafe feelings or touches, children will recognize the beginnings of sexual abuse. Although it is clearly advantageous if children can identify their feelings and take action to make themselves safe, it is unrealistic to expect this approach to stop child sexual abuse.

There are many reasons for children's difficulties in learning about this. The greatest problem of all is that, in the early stages, most child sexual abuse feels neither unsafe nor bad; on the contrary, abuse by caregivers often has its beginnings in 'good' and safe touches such as cuddles and hugs accompanied by overt favouritism, attention, flattery and treats. Older siblings and their friends often introduce sexually abusive behaviour to boys as harmless fun or 'what men normally do'.

A second hazard is that children acquire their concepts of safety from the adults in charge. If adults say, 'It's all right, there's no need to be afraid', children accept these assurances because they believe adults to be their protectors. Research has shown that these are the primary reasons why children find it difficult to identify and report sexual abuse involving trusted adults (Kraizer, 1986).

An additional danger is that children are unable to reconcile bad touching or wrong behaviour with 'good' people; that is, people they trust and those who purport to love them. Children judge the adults' worth on their face value. And when sex is presented as a sign of affection to children who are affection starved, it is unlikely to be regarded as unwanted or unsafe.

Another danger of concentrating on the touching aspects of abuse is that children associate touching with the use of hands. Unless there is a broader perspective, there is a risk that sexual abuse which does not involve hands (such as oral or anal sex) may be classified wrongly. For the touching concept to be effective as a tool for child protection, it is necessary to draw children's attention to different kinds of touching in their day-to-day environment as well as using puppets and role play to assist with the identification of sexual touching.

An additional anxiety for educators is the risk that, by identifying sexual touching as 'bad', children may acquire negative attitudes towards their own sexuality. This is why it is important that age-appropriate sexuality education is taught alongside personal safety skills. This is especially important for helping adolescents to understand about body changes, body functioning and the importance of caring sexual relationships. However, given the importance of sexuality education to children's safety, it should start long before puberty.

This part of the program is so important and so complex that teachers and parents must adopt evaluation procedures at every stage to ensure that children have learned the necessary concepts and can apply them appropriately to different situations.

Worrying (or confusing) touching

Sexual abuse may start out as a game or tickling which feels good. It can also change, making recipients unsure of whether they want the behaviour to continue or not. It is very difficult for children to stop this kind of behaviour once it is established. Child molesters take advantage of children's curiosity and confusion. Touching is worrying when it does not match our values and expectations. If the behaviour has never happened before, it may create a mixture of pleasant and unpleasant feelings. Worried feelings are especially likely to appear when children are excited by stroking in the genital area but sense that it is wrong or fear that they will get into trouble if the behaviour is discovered by other adults.

Touches become worrying when we are not really sure of the toucher's intentions. Confusion is especially likely when the toucher is saying something that contradicts the behaviour; for example, the toucher assures the victim that 'everyone does it' but, simultaneously, asks the victim to promise secrecy. There is also confusion when the perpetrator causes pain but assures the victim that what is happening is enjoyable. The victim is apt to think, 'there must be something wrong with me'.

Teaching method

- Introduce the concept of touching as outlined in the text.

- Make 'What if…' problem solving cards.

- Use slides to demonstrate good, safe, touches that people are obviously enjoying, and touching that is obviously not enjoyable. Ask children what is happening in the pictures: 'What kind of touching is it? How can you tell?'. Encourage children to relate touching to feelings. New Zealand, British and Anglo-Celt Australian children often use the word 'rude' to describe sexual behaviour and sex talk. American children may use the expression 'dirty' for the same circumstances. Find out what children know about 'rude', worrying or bad behaviour and touches. Most children have experienced these in their peer group.

- With groups, make pictorial cards showing different kinds of touching. Let children cut out pictures from magazines to supplement the text and provide further opportunities for discussion.

- Provide examples of different kinds of touches by using puppets and role plays.

- Demonstrate good touches such as hugs, pats, kisses and strokes that are clearly enjoyed by both parties. Discussion will focus on what it feels like when we get good touches that we like.

- Teach children that good touching can change to become bad, 'rude' or worrying touching and it's OK to stop it when you don't want any more. How can it be stopped?

- Include rules about safe and good touching in class safety rules.

- Advise parents of the need to promote and implement the same rules within the extended family. Efforts are wasted if, while teaching children that they have the right to reject unwanted touching at school, parents deprive them of opportunities to practise that right at home.

- Repeat simple safety guidelines whenever opportunities present themselves, such as, 'We never keep secrets about touching' or 'I think you should try to do that yourself… Adults aren't allowed to touch those special parts of your body'.

- Check that children understand the meaning of 'private'.

- Check that children know the names of the private parts of their bodies.

- Ensure that children know that no one is allowed to kiss or put anything in their mouths without their permission.

- Tell children as often as necessary that touching safety rules apply all of the time, whoever they are with. Some adults don't know about the rules for touching children, and kids have to tell them. Some men don't know, some women don't know, some big kids don't know. The rules apply at home and school, on the school bus, in a taxi…anywhere and everywhere.

- Tell children to let you know if they are unsure about the 'rightness' of touching.

- Start a class book about 'Different kinds of touching'.

- Let children know that you will help them to stop touching that they don't like.

- Ensure that children have practice in saying 'No' to adults (and each other) in a convincing way.

169

- If children need help for personal hygiene, ensure that they and staff are aware of and practice the basic rules for safe touching.[1]

Rules for touching

When talking about unacceptable touching:

- Be open and honest and admit that some children and some adults don't keep to the rules. People who give 'rude' or bad touches know that what they're doing is wrong but they do it just the same. If kids don't tell anybody about it, the people who are breaking the rules just keep on doing it, upsetting lots of children. The best way to stop them is to tell someone about it…and keep on telling people until it stops. Who can you tell?

- Check that children, parents and caregivers know the rules relating to body ownership and body privacy:
  - no tickling or touching is allowed if we say 'No'
  - no tickling or touching is allowed under our clothes
  - no one is allowed to touch the private parts of our body just for fun
  - even if a doctor needs to touch our private parts, a nurse, our mother (or a member of staff) will be there
  - no one is allowed to ask us to touch their private parts
  - if children need help with personal hygiene, their private parts should not be tickled, touched with fingers or touched for fun
  - we don't keep secrets about the private parts of bodies.

- Ensure that parents are aware of the importance of practising safety rules at home.

- Emphasize that, if someone breaks the rules, it is important to tell an adult who will listen and help. Grown-ups are not allowed to break the rules. Other kids are not allowed to break them. If they forget the rules, grown ups need to be reminded that it's wrong. If children don't tell anyone that they're getting bad or worrying touches, people will keep on breaking rules.

- Tell children (and give regular reminders) that, 'if older kids or adults do wrong or "rude" things to you, it is never your fault and you are never to blame'. Most children have experienced reprimands by parents and school staff for talking about sexual things. They know that sexual misbehaviour is naughty. They believe that it is their own fault if someone is 'rude' to them and, for that reason, they dare not report it. Children need to understand that they will not get into trouble for reporting sexual misbehaviour.

- Tell children that 'you might get a rude or bad touch anywhere at any time. You can get a bad touch in school or at home or on the way home. The person giving a bad touch might be an older person, it might be a

---

1   We recommend Eric Berg's mini booklets *Touch talk, Tell Someone* and *STOP IT* to use with this module. They are available from Network Publications, P.O. 8506, Santa Cruz, CA 95061–8506, USA and education book shops.

woman or a man. It could be someone you don't know or someone you know really well.'

- Tell children that we don't have to put up with rude, dirty or bad behaviour, and if someone breaks the rules, we must tell a responsible adult.

- Encourage children to work out who they can tell.

- Give children the opportunity to role play and practise rejecting and reporting inappropriate touching.

- Teach children that if the first person they tell doesn't listen or doesn't believe them, they must keep on telling until someone helps them to stop it; use role play and puppets to demonstrate situations in which adults ignore children.

- Use problem solving methods to encourage children to work out solutions for themselves: 'Suppose that your mum was busy and didn't listen, 'Who else could you tell?'...'Suppose that he/she didn't believe you... What could you do next?'.

AFTER EACH SESSION

Please use a formal method of evaluation to learn which children have developed the necessary concepts and which children have not.

Use puppets to seek responses for handling unwanted and inappropriate touching

When referring to inappropriate touching, adopt a third party approach wherever possible to protect group members who have already been abused.

Use a puppet to disclose a worrying problem to the audience. The puppet then refers to the fact that the children have learned about staying safe and asks for their advice.

When children become skilled at problem solving, they can be presented with different situations and puppets to work out solutions for themselves. After each story, ask the children how the puppet would have felt in the circumstances described. What could the puppet do to feel better and stay safe?

Question whether children's answers are safe. Can the respondents think of something even safer? Would the suggestion stop the unwanted behaviour? Different kinds of touching can be demonstrated by using two puppets. For example:

- Puppet A pulls Puppet B's hair and calls her rude names. The audience is asked how Puppet B might feel. Does she want to be touched like this? Does Puppet B have to put up with it? What can she do?

- A genderless puppet discloses to the audience that, when visiting a good friend, the friend's father sits the puppet on his knee and this gives him/her a worrying feeling. What can the puppet do about it?

- Puppet A is having a drink. Puppet B spills the drink down Puppet A and starts wiping it off, touching private areas of the body. Is this allowed? What can the puppet do?

- Male puppet tells the class that some big boys put their hands up his pants and he asks the class what to do.

Make workcards

Workcards can be made to help children to differentiate between good touches and touches that should be stopped.

For example, what if:

- the teacher pats you on the back and says 'Well done!'?
- your mum gives you a cuddle when she tucks you in bed?
- someone changes a baby's nappy?

What could someone do if:

- they were wrestling with the babysitter and the babysitter started to tickle them under their clothes?
- they were in the swimming pool and someone tried to pull off their trunks/swimsuit?
- an adult wanted to dry them when they came out of the shower but they'd rather do it themselves?
- someone nipped their bottom when they were getting off the bus?
- a big boy said 'I'll give you all this money if you play with my penis (willy/dick/etc.)'?

Teaching and practising reporting skills

Unless children have already been given permission to describe and report 'rude' behaviour, they will not disclose sexual abuse. Some give vague hints expecting adults to understand.

Unless they have been given opportunities to practise reporting occurrences children are unlikely to have the confidence to make a factual report. They may not even know what to say if they have never experienced such behaviour before. A great deal of practice is needed to develop accuracy in reporting. This is especially necessary when children have restricted communication skills.

Children's capacity to report can be checked by using problems such as unwanted touching or rude behaviour.

For example:

A PROBLEM WITH THE BABYSITTER

Suppose that your mum went out and left you with a new babysitter – someone you didn't know. And suppose that the babysitter said,

'I'll let you stay up late tonight and watch videos. And I've got something really special for you. But, first of all, we're going to play a new game.'

Do you like playing games? Suppose the babysitter says that, to play this game, you have to take all your clothes off. Is that a good game or a bad game?

Is it allowed?

Why?

Would you have to play the game if it was a grown-up babysitter?

Why?

NOTE TO TEACHERS

Vulnerable children will say that they know that the game is wrong but they have to obey babysitters and adults because otherwise they will get angry. Some children may say that they like playing games with babysitters and some may reveal that they have already played these kinds of games with teenage minders.

If children say that they would refuse to play, ask:

'What would you do to stay safe from someone who wanted to do 'rude' things?'.

Some children will say that they could refuse to play, tell the offender that 'it's not allowed' and go to bed. Very few children know how to contact their parents when they leave them with other people. When children know their parents' whereabouts and can contact them, they exhibit more confidence, even in role play.

Should you tell someone about this?

Is it an emergency or not an emergency? Why?

Who would you tell?

When would you tell?

What would you say?

Most children respond that they would tell their mothers but, when asked what they would say, they use vague expressions such as, 'I don't like the babysitter' or 'The babysitter is mean'.

If children respond in this way, use further questioning.

'Would your mummy know what the babysitter had done if you said that...?'

'Would your mummy want the babysitter to do that to you?'

Children invariably confirm that their mothers would not want to employ babysitters who behave rudely because 'it's not allowed'.

'OK. Let's start again. If someone wants you to do something that isn't allowed and you want that person to stop, what can you do to make sure that they don't do it again?

What could you say to the person?

What could you say to your mother?

Suppose that your mummy wasn't listening? Suppose that she's watching TV and just says, 'Umm'. What else can you do?'

Pursue this line of questioning until children report exactly what happened and indicate that, if mother didn't listen, they could tell others, including teachers, police and social workers. If children say that they would telephone police or a relative ask them to demonstrate how they would make the call and role play to assist the conversation. Children need the confidence to disclose problems in an open and honest way.

We touch things all the time

Touching is something that we do all the time.
We are touching every hour of every day.
We touch the sheets when we're asleep in bed.
We touch our clothes when we get dressed in the morning.
We touch the food that we eat.
In fact we never stop touching.
We touch things with all the different parts of our bodies.
What are you touching right now?

What are your feet touching?

What is your left hand touching?

What is your right elbow touching?

What are your buttocks touching?

Some touching feels good.

Some touching feels bad.

Tell me about the touching that feels good – the touching that you like.

Start a class book on 'Different Kinds of Touching'.

WORKSHEET

I LOOK GOOD TOUCHES!

Good touches are great! I like lots and lots of them. These are the good touches that I like

_____

_____

_____

_____

_____

This is a picture of somebody who gives me good touches that I like.

My good toucher is called _____

And this is how I like to be touched_____

_____

_____

_____

_____

GOOD TOUCHES CAN CHANGE TO BAD TOUCHES

Most touches are good touches.
We all like good touches.
But sometimes, good touches change and become bad touches.
Bad touches can hurt.
Bad touches can feel yukky.
Bad touches are worrying.
We want them to stop.

These are the bad touches that I don't like _ _ _ _ _ _ _ _ _ _ _ _

_ _

_ _

_ _

_ _

_ _

_ _

_ _

And the people who give bad touches are called _ _ _ _ _ _ _ _ _

_ _

_ _

_ _

_ _

_ _

_ _

_ _

There are cheek hugs

and arm hugs

There are side to side hugs

and quick hugs

There are lots of different kinds of hugs. Do you like to be hugged?

And sometimes there are even group hugs

Group Hugs

Rules for hugging

There are good hugs and bad hugs.
Good hugs are great!
Have you ever had a good hug?
Who gives you good hugs?

Sometimes, we don't want to be hugged.
Nobody wants to be hugged all the time.
So, we have to have rules about hugging.

You can only hug people if you know that they
want to be hugged.
And if you give a good hug that someone
likes, there's a very good chance that
the person will hug you too.

What can you do if someone wants to give
you a big bear hug and you don't feel like it?

Look at this picture of a blind boy being helped to cross the road.

Is the boy getting good touches he likes or bad touches he wants to stop?

Here is a picture of a boy who is just getting into the bath.

Is this a good touch that he likes or a bad touch that he wants to stop?

How can you tell?

Swinging can be fun!

But it's a bad touch
if someone pushes you too high
and you want to get off

Tickling can hurt

Tickling can be fun. Tickling can make us laugh.

But sometimes, we don't want to be tickled.
Sometimes the tickling goes on for too long and it hurts.

When you want the tickling to stop, say 'No. Stop it!' in a big loud voice. Try saying, 'No'.
Even louder ! Louder still, as if you really mean it !
Now, once more but, this time, sit up straight and look me straight in the eye while you say, 'No'

Is this a good touch or a bad touch?

How can you tell?

Is this a good touch or a bad touch?

How can you tell?

What should the girl do?

Touching that hurts

There are rules about touching.

> Keep away from bad touches.
> Never give bad touches to other people.
> Bad touches can hurt.
> Bad touches make people feel bad.
> Let's see how many hurting touches you know about.

Brainstorm and make a list of 'Touching that hurts' and add 'Touches that hurt' to the class book.

Role play: 'Would you like me to brush your hair?'

One adult takes the part of the parent and mother and another (preferably with long hair) takes the part of a female child.

Commence action: The child is trying to brush her hair when the parent comes into the room. The child is tugging at her hair and looks uncomfortable.

> 'Would you like me to do that?' asks the parent.

> 'Ooh, yes please', says the child.

Stop action: ask the audience whether this gives the child a good feeling or a bad feeling. How can they tell?

Resume action: The child hands the brush to the parent who begins to brush gently.

> The child comments that it feels good and she looks happy.
> The audience is then asked whether the child is having a good or a bad feeling: Is this a good touch or a bad touch?

> The adult then pretends that the hair is knotted and she brushes harder. The child's facial expressions give the impression that she is in pain.

Stop action: Ask if this is still a good touch. What kind of touch is it? Can X (the child) do anything to stop it? What can he/she do?

Resume action: The child begins to twitch and complain. The adult gets angry and tells the child to sit still because twitching only makes the brushing hurt. The child continues to move away from the brush and the adult gets very cross.

Stop action: 'Is X (the child) having good feelings or bad feelings? Is this a good touch or a bad touch?'

> 'Do you think that X (the child) knows that her head is part of her body. Who owns her body? Do you think she knows that she doesn't have to be touched in ways that make her feel uncomfortable?

What can she do to get rid of those bad feelings?

Do you think that we should tell her?

Stop action: Teacher addresses the child:

'We would like to know how you feel right now. Is it a good feeling or a bad feeling?

Do you want that feeling to stop?'

The person taking the part of the child says that she wants it to stop 'but you can't stop grown-ups'.

The teacher addresses the audience and asks, 'Is she right?'

Teacher to 'child':

'Did you know that your body is your own body?' It's no one else's. When grown-ups touch you in uncomfortable ways, you can tell them that you don't like it. Why don't you give it a try to see what happens'.

It may be useful for the child to ask the class/group to help:

'You seem to know a lot about it. Is my body really my own? What should I do?'

In the discussion, the teacher should ensure that X (the child) is informed that she should tell the adult that she doesn't like the touching from the very first moment that she feels uncomfortable.

After discussion, the scene should be repeated. The teacher asks the children in the audience to help X to say, 'No' at the precise moment that the brushing becomes uncomfortable. Help the audience to work out when the good touch changes and becomes a bad touch. The teacher instructs each child to call out 'Now' at the precise moment when X looks uncomfortable. The person acting the part of the child will then tell the parent that the brushing hurts: 'No! Please don't brush so hard. It hurts and I don't like it!

The parent then apologizes and brushes more gently.

The audience is asked whether the child and the parent now have good or bad feelings.

This scene is extremely useful for demonstrating that good touches can turn to bad touches and that good feelings can change and become bad feelings. Furthermore, just because we said 'Yes' in the beginning, does not mean that we can't change our minds. The role play tells children that it is best to say 'No! I don't like that!' as soon as the touch changes from good to bad.

Some touches give yukky feelings

Some touches give yukky feelings.
When someone sits you on their
knee and you don't want to be
there, you get a yukky feeling.

When someone wants to
give you a big, wet,
sloppy, kiss you get a
yukky feeling.

Some cuddles are yukky too!

When someone gives you a yukky touch, just remember, it's YOUR body. You can say 'No' and move away. And if the yukky person doesn't take any notice, ask an adult to help you. Who could you ask? What would you say?

Yukky touches can be worrying

Some people give yukky touches.

Yukky touches can be worrying.
Sometimes, we're not really sure what to do when we get a yukky touch.
Sometimes, it starts out as a good touch that we like and then it becomes yukky.
Yukky touches are worrying if no one has ever touched us like that before.
Can you think of a yukky touch?

Some people give yukky touches and think it's fun.
We should never give a 'yukky' touch.
Try not to get one!

Sexual touches

Rude (wrong or bad) touches are the hardest touches to talk about.
It's worrying if someone wants us to do something rude (naughty or dirty).
If someone does rude or wrong things to us, that's worrying too.
Kids should only get good touches.
If touching worries YOU, just remember, it's your body, you're the boss. You don't have to put up with bad (rude) touching.

Say, 'No! Stop that! It's not allowed'. Move away as fast as you can and tell somebody about it. Who can you tell?

If someone touches the private parts of your body it isn't your fault

It's never your fault if someone does rude (or dirty) things to you.
Some kids do it.
Some grownups do it.
They know it's wrong, but they do it just the same.
No one is allowed to touch the private places on your body.
No one is allowed to touch your breasts if you're a girl.
No one is allowed to put their hands in your pants.
No one is allowed to put your hand in their pants.
Private parts are private and we keep them covered up.

Remember, it's your body. You're the boss.
So, if someone's rude (or does wrong things) to you, tell your teacher.
Tell a grown-up who will listen and help.
And keep on telling until they listen and help.
You will feel much better if you tell
Who could you tell?

And if you know someone who is worried about bad behaviour, tell them that people aren't allowed to do these things with kids. Listen to what they have to say and help them to tell an adult who will help.

No touching for fun!

No one is allowed to touch
the private parts of your
body just for fun.

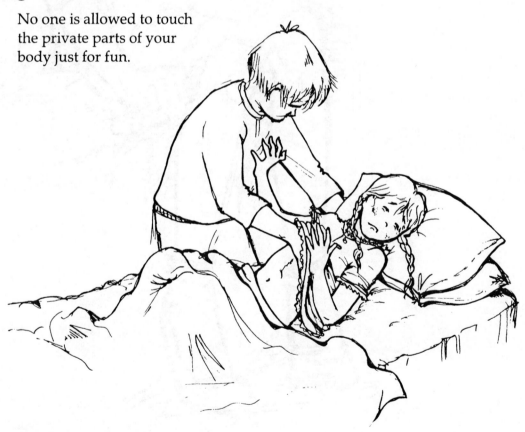

No one is allowed to tickle
you under your clothes.

No one is allowed to mess
around with the private parts of your body.

No one is allowed to peep at your private places just for fun. They're private. That's why we cover them with clothes.

And no one should show their
private parts of their body
to you.

Point to the private parts of your body.

Some people don't know the rules about touching

Some people don't know the rules about touching.
Sometimes big kids do things that are not allowed.
Sometimes, grown-ups don't know how to behave with kids.
And sometimes little kids have to tell big people to stop.

No! Stop that!
It's my body.
I don't like it.

No! Stop that!
It's not allowed

Then tell someone who will help.

Reporting secrets

Suppose that a grown-up person you know behaved rudely to you and then said,

'Don't you ever tell anybody about this. If you do, you'll get into big trouble. It's our special secret.'

Do you have to keep secrets?

Which secrets can you tell?

Is this a good secret or a bad one?

Would you really get into trouble for telling a bad secret?

Are grown-ups allowed to do rude things to kids and tell them to keep it secret?

What could you do?

Who could you tell?

What could you say?

Suppose that the person did't believe you and thought you were making it up? How many people could you tell?

When could you stop telling?

Andrew had a problem with a big boy at school. He was a bully who pushed kids around. Andrew was scared of going to the toilet in case the big boy was there. He tried to wait until he got home but sometimes he left it too late and wet his pants.

Mum was cross 'You're too old to be doing this, she said. 'I'm tired of washing your pants.' Andrew tried to tell mum about the big boy but she was busy washing the pants and she was very, very grumpy.

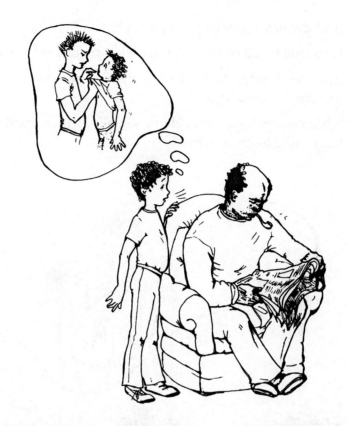

When dad came home from work, mum told him that Andrew had wet his pants. Dad told him off for being lazy.

'There's a big boy…' said Andrew, but dad wasn't listening, he was reading the paper.

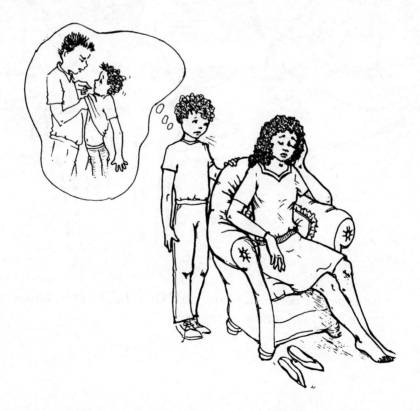

Then Andrew's sister came home from school. She started to tease him. Andrew said, 'I don't like school toilets' – but she was watching TV.

Andrew has a problem with a big boy.

He needs to tell someone about it but no one is listening. What can he do?

Andrew decided to wait until they all sat down to eat and then, in a big important voice, he said,

'Listen mum. Listen dad. I have something important to tell you. This is what's happening to me at school'.

And they all listened. Mum said 'That shouldn't be happening'. Dad said 'I'll come to school with you tomorrow'.

WORKSHEET

If someone told me to keep a bad secret, these are the people that I could tell:

_____

and _____

and _____

and if they didn't believe me, this is what I could do:

_____

_____

_____

_____

_____

_____

_____

Ways of Integrating Personal Safety into the Curriculum

The following are ideas for the integration of personal safety education into other curriculum subjects.

Health
Sex Education ⎤
Drug Education ⎥ at the appropriate developmental level
AIDS Education ⎦
Safety with medicines
General safety
Growing and caring for each other
Personal hygiene

Crafts
Make puppets, group collages, posters
Make safety badges
Painting, colouring
Surveying and making plans of the local government

Music
Songs relating to our bodies and safety

Language Arts
Stories about children who solve problems and stay safe
Practice in problem solving
Practice in brainstorming

Maths
Pictorial representation (e.g. graphs, histograms) relating to individual differences

Social Studies
Investigate/invite police, child protection and support services
Invite representatives from organizations providing information and services relating to the disabilities of children

Drama
Puppetry
Role Play

Communications
Teach children about emergency services and how to use telephones and make contact without adult help.

Other Resources for the Protection of Children with Disabilities

The ABCD Pack: Abuse and Children Who are Disabled

Leicester: NSPCC. 1994. A kit relating to the protection of deaf children.

Circles II: Stop Abuse

Teaching self protection skills to persons with developmental disabilities (Marklyn Champagne, Leslie Walker – Hirsh, 1986 published by James Stanfield Publishing Co., PO 41058B. Santa Barbara CA 93140).

A program based on the USA version of the Circle Concept that deals with issues of inappropriate touching from friends and strangers.

This works well with the Australian version of the Circle Concept (Susie Smith) or separately as an anti-victim training programme. Price $399 US + postage (1991).

Personal Safety Program

Avoiding Sexual Abuse by Rosemary Reed and Nesta Spillane, Threads, (1989) PO.43, Mandurah WA 6210. A kit designed by teachers as part of the Health Education Syllabus for middle primary level school children. Price $510 A. (1991).

No-Go-Tell

A kit by Elizabeth Krents of the Lexington Center Child Abuse and Disability Program, 1986 for very young disabled children aged 3–7. It teaches fundamental prevention concepts using 55 illustrations and anatomically correct dolls.

Available from James Stanfield Inc. Price $299 US (1991).

Safe and Okay

By Stella Brener and Elizabeth Krents and similar to 'No-Go-Tell'. The kit caters for older children (grades 3–6) with communicative impairments and developmental disabilities. Price $325 US (1991).

Curriculum for developing an awareness of sexual exploitation and teaching self protection techniques

By Ellen Ryersen (1977) from the Developmental Disabilities Project of Seattle Rape Relief. 1825 So. Jackson, Suite 102, Seattle, Washington 98144 USA.

Visual materials and lesson plans. The curriculum requires between 3 and 6 months of instruction increasing to one year. A revision of the K-12 Curriculum is also available.

Special Education Curriculum and Sexual Exploitation

This is for people aged 6 years to adults with developmental disabilities.

Audio tapes $56 US for Level 1 age 6–11 years and Level 2, age 12–adult $495 US (1991) from CHEF, 20832 Pacific Highway South, Seattle, Washington 98188, USA.

Child Protection Curriculum – for preventing child sexual assault of students with intellectual disability

New South Wales Department of School Education, 1989. Curriculum Statement and support materials.

Bibliography

Abel, G.G., Becker, J.V., Mittelman, M.S., Cunningham-Rathner, J., Rouleau, J.L., Murphy, W.D. (1987) 'Self-reported sex crimes of non-incarcerated paraphiliacs'. *Journal of Interpersonal Violence, 2,* 6 3–25.

Adams, C. (1986) 'Considering children's developmental stages in prevention education'. In M. Nelson and K. Clark (eds) *The educator's guide to preventing child sexual abuse.* Santa Cruz, CA: Network Publications.

Ammerman, R.T., Van Haslett, V.B., Hersen, M., McGonigle, J.J., and Lubetsky, M.J. (1989) 'Abuse and neglect in psychiatrically hospitalized multihandicapped children'. *Child Abuse and Neglect, 13,* 335–343.

Anderson, C. (1982) *Teaching People with Mental Retardation about Sexual Abuse Prevention.* Minneapolis: Illusion Theater Guide.

Anderson, C. (1986) 'A history of the touch continuum.' In M. Nelson and R. Clark (eds) *The educator's guide to preventing child sexual abuse.* Santa Cruz, CA: Network Publications.

Bagley, C. and King, K. (1990) *Child sexual abuse: The search for healing.* London: Tavistock/Routledge.

Bentovim, A. (1991) 'Evaluation of a comprehensive treatment approach to child sexual abuse within the family'. Paper presented to the Third European Conference on Child Abuse and Neglect, Prague.

Berrick, J. (1988) 'Parent involvement in child abuse prevention training. What do they learn?' *Child Abuse and Neglect, 12,* 543–553.

Blomberg, P.S. (1986) 'Vulnerability issues of children with developmental disabilities: Sexual exploitation, the problem, solutions and assessments'. Paper presented at Current Issues for Child Abuse Professionals Conference, December. Cited in Senn (1988).

Barnados (North East) (1987) *Family Placement Project Child Sexual Abuse Training Programme for Foster Parents with Teenage Placements.* Barnados, July.

Briere, J., Runtz, M. (1989) '"University males" sexual interest in children – Predicting indices of 'pedophilia' in a non-forensic sample.' *Child Abuse and Neglect, 13,* 1, 65–76.

Briggs, F. (1986) *Child Sexual Abuse – Confronting The Problem.* Melbourne: Pitman.

Briggs, F. (1987) 'South Australian Parents Want Child Protection Programs To Be Offered In Schools and Preschools.' *Australian Journal of Early Childhood, 12,* 1. *Reproduced in Early Child Development and Care, 34,* 167–178, 1988.

Briggs, F., Lehmann, K. (1989) 'Significance of children's drawings in cases of sexual abuse.' *Early Child Development and Care, 47*, 131–147; and paper presented to the Eighth International Congress on Child Abuse and Neglect, Hamburg, September 1990.

Briggs, F. (1991a) 'Child protection programs: Can they protect children?' *Early Child Development and Care, 67*, 61–72.

Briggs, F. (1991b) 'Keeping Ourselves Safe: A personal safety curriculum examined.' *Set* No. 2 Item 7, New Zealand Council for Educational Research, Wellington, NZ.

Briggs, F. (1993) *Why my child?* Sydney: Allen and Unwin.

Briggs, F. (1994a) *Developing personal safety skills in children with disabilities.* Paper presented to the 1st National Intervention Conference, Adelaide, Australia 14–16 March.

Briggs, F. (Ed) (1995) *From Victim to Offender.* Sydney: Allen and Unwin.

Briggs, F. and Hawkins, R.M. (1993a) 'Children's perceptions of personal safety issues and their vulnerability to molestation.' *Children Australia, 18*, 3, 4–9.

Briggs, F. and Hawkins, R.M. (1993b) 'Follow-up data on the effectiveness of New Zealand's national school based child protection program.' *Child Abuse and Neglect, 18*,8, 635–643.

Briggs, F. and Hawkins, R.M. (1994a) *A comparison of the early childhood and family experiences of (a) convicted, incarcerated male child molesters and (b) men who were sexually abused in childhood who have no convictions for offences against children.* Report for the Criminology Research Council, Canberra. University of South Australia.

Briggs, F. and Hawkins, R.M. (1994b) 'Follow-up study of children of 5–8 years using child protection programs in Australia and New Zealand.' *Early Child Development and Care, 100*, 111–117.

Brown, H. and Craft, A. (eds) *Thinking the unthinkable: Papers on sexual abuse and people with learning difficulties* (29–38) London: Family Planning Association Education Unit.

Budin, L.E. and Johnson, C.F. (1989) 'Sex Abuse prevention Programs – Offenders' Attitudes'. *Child Abuse and Neglect, 13*, 77–89.

Cavanagh Johnson, T. (1988) 'Child perpetrators – children who molest other children: Preliminary findings.' *Child Abuse and Neglect, 12*, 219–229.

Chamberlain, A., Rauh, J., Passer, A., McGrath, M. and Burket, R. (1984) 'Issues in fertility control for mentally retarded female adolescents: I. Sexual activity, sexual abuse and contraception'. *Pediatrics, 73*, 4, 445–450.

Conte, J.R. and Berliner, L. (1981) 'Sexual abuse of children: Implications for practice.' *Social Casework, 62*, 601–606.

Conte, J.R., Rosen, C., Saperstein, L. and Shermack, R. (1985) 'An evaluation of a program to prevent the sexual victimization of young children.' *Child Abuse and Neglect, 9*, 319–328.

Conte, J.R. (1986) *A Look at Child Sexual Abuse.* Chicago: National Committee for Prevention of Child Abuse.

Cook, M. and Howells, K. (1981) *Adult sexual interest in children.* London: Academic Press.

Craft, A. (ed) (1987) *Health, social and sexual education for children, adolescents and adults with a mental handicap: A review of resources.* London: Health Education Authority.

Craft, A. and Craft, M. (1978) *Sex and the mentally handicapped.* London: Routledge and Kegan Paul.

Craft, A. and Hitching, M. (1989) 'Keeping safe: Sex education and assertiveness skills.' In R. Dawson (1984) *The Abuse of Children in Foster Care: A study of incidence, characteristics and precipitating characters.* Toronto: Ontario Association of Children's Aid Societies.

Downer, A. (1984) *Evaluation of talking about touching.* Seattle, WA: Committee for Children. *ERIC Clearinghouse on Handicapped and Gifted Children*, Digest # 446 1987.

204

Fenton, M. and Hughes, P. (1989) *Passivity To Empowerment – a living skills curriculum for people with disabilities.* London: The Royal Association for Disability and Rehabilitation.

Finkelhor, D. (1981) 'Survey of parents in Boston conducted under a grant from the National Centre for the Prevention and Control of Rape.' Cited in D. Finkelhor (1984) *Child sexual abuse – New theory and research.* New York: Free Press.

Finkelhor, D. (1979) *Sexually victimized children,* New York: Free Press.

Finkelhor, D. (1984) *Child sexual abuse: New theory and research.* New York: Free Press.

Finkelhor, D. (1986) *A Source of Child Sexual Abuse.* New York: Sage Publications.

Finkelhor, D. and Araji, S. (1983) *The prevention of child sexual abuse: A review of current approaches.* SAPR, 17, 21st December.

Finkelhor, D. and Araji, S. (1986) 'Explanations of Paedophilia – a four factor model.' *The Journal of Sex Research, 22,* 145–161.

Finkelhor, D. and Browne, A. (1985) 'The traumatic impact of child sexual abuse: a conceptualization.' *American Journal of Orthopsychiatry, 55,* 4, 530–541.

Finkelhor, D. and Strapko, I.M. (1987) 'Sexual Abuse Prevention Education'. Paper prepared for inclusion in D. J. Willis, E. M. Holl, and M. Rosenberg, (eds) *Child Abuse Prevention.* New York: Wiley.

Finkelhor, D., Asdigian, N. and Dziuba-Leatherman, J. (1993) *Victimization Prevention Training in Action: A national survey of children's experiences coping with actual threats and assaults.* New Hampshire: University of New Hampshire.

Forchuk, C., Pitkeathly, F., Cook, D., Allen, J. and St. Denis McDonald, R.N. (1984) 'Sex education and the mentally retarded.' *Canadian Nurse, 80,* 36–39.

Garbarino, J., Stott, F.M. (1989) *What Can Children Tell Us?* New York: Jossey Bass.

Garbarino, J., Brookhauser, P.E., Authier, K.J. and Associates (1987) *Special Children, Special Risks: The Maltreatment of children with disabilities.* New York: Aldine D.E. Gruyter.

Gilbert, N., Berrick, J.D., Le Prohn, N. and Nijman, N. (1989) *Protecting children from sexual abuse: does pre-school training work?* University of New Hampshire: Family Research Lab.

Goldman, R. and Goldman, J. (1988) *Show Me Yours.* Melbourne: Penguin.

Goodman, L. (1973) 'The sexual rights of the retarded – A dilemma for parents.' *The Family Coordinator, 22,* 472–474.

Hard, S. (1986) *Sexual Abuse of the Developmentally Disabled: a case study.* Paper presented at the National Conference of Executives of Associations for Retarded Citizens, Omaha, Nebraska, October. Cited in Senn (1988).

Hindman, J. (undated) *Abuses to sexual abuse prevention programs or ways we abuse our children as we attempt to prevent abuse.* Canada: Alexandra Associates. Cited in Mayes *et al.* (1990).

Hunter, M. (1990) *Abused boys: the neglected victims of sexual abuse.* New York: Fawcett Columbine.

Kennedy, A.E.C. (1973) 'The effects of deafness on personality – A discussion based on the theoretical model of Erikson's Eight Stages of Man'. *Journal of the Rehabilitation of the Deaf, 6,* 3, 22–33.

Kennedy, M. (1989) 'The abuse of deaf children.' *Child Abuse Review,* Spring, 3–7.

Kennedy, M. (1990) *The deaf child who is sexually abused – Is there a need for a dual specialist?* London: National Deaf Society.

Kennedy, M. (1990a) 'No more secrets – please.' In *Deafness 90,* Journal of the National Council of Social Workers with Deaf People and the British Deaf Association, 1, 6, 10–12.

Kennedy, M. (1991) '*Elements of Therapy*'. Unpublished paper from the National Deaf Society (UK).

Klepsch, M. (1982) *Children draw and tell*. New York: Brunner/Mazel Inc.

Kraizer, S.K. (1986) 'Rethinking prevention'. *Child Abuse and Neglect, 10,* 259–261.

Krivacska, J.J. (1990) *Designing child sexual abuse prevention programs: Current approaches and a proposal for the prevention, reduction and identification of sexual misuse*. Springfield IL: Charles C. Thomas.

Lewis, D. and Greene, J. (1983) *Your child's drawings, their hidden meaning*. London: Hutchinson & Co. Ltd.

Longo, R.E., Gochenour, C. (1981) 'Sexual Assault of handicapped individuals.' *Journal of Rehabilitation, 47,* 24–27.

MacFarlane, K. and Waterman, J. (1986) *Sexual abuse of young children*. New York: The Guilford Press.

Mayes, G.M., Currie, E.F., MacLeod, L., Gillies, J.B., Warden, D.A. (1992) *Child sexual abuse*. Edinburgh: Scottish Academic Press.

Meadow, K.P. (1980) *Deafness and child development*. Berkley, CA: University of California Press.

Mindel, E.D. and Vernon, M. (eds) (1987) *They grow in silence* (2nd edition). Boston, MA: Little Brown.

Mitchell, L.K. (1985) *Behavioural Intervention in the Sexual Problems of Mentally Handicapped Individuals: In residential and home settings*. Springfield, IL: Charles C. Thomas.

Moglia, R. (1986) 'Sexual Abuse and Disability.' *SIECUS Report*, March 9–10, 1986.

Monat-Haller, R. (1992) *Understanding and expressing sexuality: Responsible choices for individuals with developmental disabilities*. Baltimore: Paul H. Brookes Publishing Co.

Moore, D.F., Weiss, K.L. and Goodwin, M.W. (1973) *Exceptional Children, 40,* 1, 22–28.

Morgenstern, M. (1973) 'Community attitudes toward sexuality of the retarded.' In F. .F de la Cruz and G. D La Vecks (eds) *Human sexuality and the Mentally Retarded*. New York: Brunner/Mazel.

Mounty, J.L., Fetterman, R.J. (1989) 'An abuse prevention program for deaf and hard of hearing children. Paper presented to the CAID Convention, San Diego, California, June 25–29.

Musick, J.L. (1984) 'Patterns of institutional sexual assault.' *Response to Violence in the Family and Sexual Assault, 7,* 3, 1–2, 10–11.

O'Day, B. (1989) *Preventing Sexual Abuse of Persons With Disabilities*. Santa Cruz, CA: Network Publications.

O.P.C.S. Survey of Disability Report number 3, *The prevalence of disability among children*. London: HMSO.

PACER (Parent Advocacy Coalition for Educational Rights) (1986) *A Resource Manual on Child Abuse*. Minneapolis: PACER.

Phoenix, S. (1987) 'Food for thought'. *Talk Magazine*. National Deaf Society, Spring.

Piaget, J. (1965) *The moral judgment of the child*. NY: Free Press.

Plummer, C.A. (1984) *Preventing sexual abuse, activities and strategies for those working with children and adolescents*. Holmes Beach, FL: Learning Publications.

Plummer, C.A. (1986) 'Child sexual abuse programs: keys to programs success.' In M. Nelson and R. Clark (eds) *The educator's guide to preventing child sexual abuse*. Santa Cruz, CA: Network Publications.

Rose, L. (1986) 'Sexual assault in special needs population.' *SIECUS Report, 1,* 1, 20–26.

Rush, F. (1980) *The Best Kept Secret: Sexual Abuse of Children*. New York: McGraw Hill Book Co.

Russell, D.E.H. (1986) 'The incest legacy: Why today's abused children become tomorrow's victims of rape.' *The Sciences*, March–April, 28–32.

Ryan, G., Lane, S., Davis, J., Isaac, C. (1987) 'Juvenile sex offenders – Development and correction.' *Child Abuse and Neglect, 2*, 385–395.

Ryan, R. (1992) 'Post traumatic stress syndrome: Assessing and treating the aftermath of sexual assault.' *Crossing new borders: Proceedings of the Ninth Annual Conference of the National Association for the Dually Diagnosed,* 8–11.

Saslawsky, D.A., Wurtele, S.K. (1986) 'Educating children about sexual abuse, implications for pediatric intervention and possible intervention.' *Journal of Pediatric Psychology, 1,* 235–245.

Sanford, T.L. (1980) *The silent children.* Garden City, NY: McGraw Hill Paperbacks.

Sank, C. and LaFleche, E. (1981) 'Special sisters: health issues for mentally retarded women.' *Off Our Backs,* May, 26.

Saphira, M. (1985) *The sexual abuse of children.* Auckland, N.Z.: Mental Health Foundation.

Saphira, M. (1987) *For your child's sake: understanding sexual abuse.* Auckland, N.Z.: Reed Methuen.

Seattle Rape Relief (1984) *Sexual Exploitation of Handicapped Students.* Developmental Disabilities Project.

Sengstock, W.L. and Vergason, G.A. (1970) 'Issues in sex education for the retarded.' *Education and Training of the Mentally Retarded, 5,* 99–103.

Senn, C.Y. (1988) *Vulnerable: Sexual abuse and people with an intellectual handicap.* Downsville, Ontario, Canada: G. Allan Roeher Institute.

Schroeder, C. (1994) 'Parents can help prevent sexual abuse of your children.' The Brown University: *Child and Adolescent Behavior Letter, 10,* 4.

Sobsey, D. (1988) 'Research on sexual abuse: Are we asking the right questions?' *Newsletter of the American Association on Mental Retardation, 2,* 2.

Sobsey, D. (1994) *Violence and abuse in the lives of people with disabilities – the end of silent acceptance.* Baltimore: Paul H. Brookes.

Sobsey, D. and Doe, T. (1991) 'Patterns of sexual abuse and assault.' *Journal of Sexuality and Disability, 9,* 3, 243–259.

Sobsey, D. and Mansell, S. (1990). 'The prevention of sexual abuse of people with developmental disabilities.' *Developmental Disabilities Bulletin, 18,* 2, 51–66.

Sullivan, P.M., Vernon, M. and Scanlan, J.M. (1987) 'Sexual abuse of deaf youth.' *American Annals of the Deaf, 132,* 4, 258–262.

Sullivan, P.M., Brookhauser, P.E., Scanlan, J.M., Knutson, J.F. and Schulte, L.E. (1991) 'Patterns of physical and sexual abuse of communicatively handicapped children.' *Annals of Otology, Rhinology and Laryngology, 100,* 3, 188–194.

Tobin, P. and Farley, S.L. (1990) *Keeping Kids Safe, A child sexual abuse prevention manual.* Holmes Beach, FL.: Learning Publications.

Tong, L., Oates, K., McDowell, M. (1987) 'Personality development following sexual abuse.' *Child Abuse and Neglect, 2,* 3, 371–384.

Turk, V. and Brown, H. (1992) *Sexual abuse of adults with learning disabilities.* Paper presented at the Conference of the International Association for Scientific Study of Mental deficiency, Brisbane, August.

Varley, C.K. (1984) 'Schizophreniform psychoses in mentally retarded adolescent girls following sexual assault.' *American Journal of Psychiatry, 141,* 4, 593–594.

Watson, A.J., Valtin, R. (1993) *It's not telling you mum, only your friend – children's understanding of secrets.* St. George's Papers in Education, Sydney, University of New South Wales, No. 2. November.

Watson, J.D. (1984) 'Talking About The Best Kept Secret – Sexual Abuse and Children with Disabilities.' *The Exceptional Parent*, September, 15–20.

Weekes, P. and Westwood, M. (1993) 'Parents deluded on teen sex lives'. *The Australian*, 31st August, p.3.

Westcott, H. (1991) 'The abuse of disabled children: A review of the literature.' *Child Care, Health and Development, 17*, 243–258.

Wurtele, S.K., Saslawsky, D., Miller, C., Marrs, S., Britcher, J. (1986) 'Teaching personal safety skills for potential prevention of sexual abuse: A comparison of treatments.' *Journal of Consulting and Clinical Psychology, 54*, 688–692.

Wurtele, S.K. (1987). 'School based sexual abuse prevention programs. A review.' *Child Abuse and Neglect, 11*, 483–495.

Wurtele, S.K. (1993) 'Enhancing children's sexual development through child sexual abuse prevention programs.' *Journal of Sex Education and Therapy, 19*, 1, 37–46.

Yaffe, M., and Nelson, E.C. (eds) (1982) *The influence of Pornography on Behaviour.* London: Academic Press.

Yates, A., Butler, L.E. and Grago, M. (1985) 'Drawings by child victims of incest.' *Child Abuse and Neglect, 9*, 183–189.

Subject Index

References in italic indicate pictures or worksheets.

ABCD Pack 209
abuse cycles 11, 44
accidental disclosure of abuse 61–2
adults
    children's assessment of 5, 20–1, 51, 168
    collusion over disclosures 22–3
    uncomfortable 30, 42
affection
    'inhibition of free expression' fears 41
    sexual abuse presented as 7, 168
'age appropriateness' queries 40
aims of programs 36
'alarming unnecessarily' fears 39
anatomical names, use of 6, 40
angry feelings 26, 70, *156*
anuses, privacy training 132
anxieties *see* fears
argument avoidance 90
assertiveness skills development 60–1, 90–5, 157
    body privacy training 121, 133–6, *133, 134, 135, 136*

assessment process, abuse reports 67–8
attention seeking strategies, teaching deaf children 53–4
Australia
    child protection programs 4, 13, 30
    research 8–9, 10, 14, 22, 31, 39
'authority challenge' fears *see* obedience issues
Avoiding Sexual Abuse program 201

babysitters 47–8, 172–3
bad feelings 141–2, *147, 148, 152, 164*
    see also 'yukky' feelings
blaming victims 10, 44
bodies, children's curiosity about 5, 16
body awareness training 57, 104–21
    'difference' activities 105–16, *106–12, 113, 117, 119*
    group activities 105
    related activities 105
body changes, with worrying feelings 139–40, *152*, 157
body language training 90
body parts, naming 124, *125–8*
body privacy training 122–37, 190–4
    introducing concept 123
    naming body parts 124, *125–8*
    private places 129–32
    rules 132–3
    saying 'no' 133–6, *133–6*
    touching 190–4, *190–4*
'body' songs 114–16
'boys are safe' myth 44
brainstorming methods 60, 64, 142

breasts, privacy training 131
bullies, saying 'no' to 92–4, 196–8, *196–8*
buttocks, privacy training 132

Canada, child protection program 3–4, 40–1
CARE Kit 3–4, 40–1
caregivers
    choice of 99, 122
    as offenders 20–1
    see also parents
Child Abuse Research and Education (CARE) Kit 3–4, 40–1
child protection programs 3–16
    effectiveness 12–14
    examples 201–2
    origins 3–4
    reasons for 4–16
choices, and independence 56
Circles II: Stop Abuse training 201
class newspapers 78
collusion, by adults 22–3, 51
Columbus Child Assault Prevention Project (CAPP) 3
communication
    barriers to effective 23–5, 54
    parent–child 45–6
    school–home 31–4
    training in 63
communication subjects, integrating safety into 200
community, safety in the 97, 103
confidence-building *see* self-esteem development

confusing (worrying)
    feelings 138–40, 157–8,
    158, 159–60
    and touching 168, 189, *189*
confusing (worrying)
    touching 168
confusion, children's 8,
    20–1, 26, 40
craft subjects, integrating
    safety into 200
cross-age tutoring 78
cuddling *see* hugging
curriculum development
    49–64
    challenges of disabled
        children 50–4
    example materials 202
    independence
        development 55–8
    integration into
        individual subjects
        200
    levels 49–50
    pace of development
        58–61
    positive environment
        61–2
    self-esteem development
        54–5
    teaching 62–4

damage caused by abuse 11,
    25–6, 38, 44
dangerous situations 98, 99
'dangerous strangers' 8–9,
    37, 47
dark, fears of the 139, 162
deaf children 17–18, 23–5,
    52–4, 66
    shortage of therapists 72
deaf cultural values 25
decision-making practice
    62–3
denial, as barrier to therapy
    71
dependence *see*
    independence

development, damage to
    children's 11, 25–6, 44
developmental disabilities
    see intellectually
    disabled children
'deviant sex' fears 40
'differences in bodies'
    activities 105–12,
    106–12, 113, 117, 119
disabilities, children with
    greater risk of abuse
        17–27
    implications 27–8
    misconceptions about
        25–6, 43, 44, 45
    special challenges 50–4
disclosure of abuse *see*
    reporting abuse
'distrust' fears 40–1
Down syndrome children 18
drama subjects, integrating
    safety into 200
drawing activities 79

emergency procedures 62,
    91, 100–2, *101*
emotional problems,
    disabled children 26, 44
emotions *see* feelings
empowering language 91
ETR Network Publications
    (USA) 46
'exaggerated problem'
    myth 42
exercise programs 57

'fabrication of allegations'
    fears 41, 43
fathers, involvement in
    programs 31–2
fears
    children's 8, 139, 99, 151,
        151, 153–4
    parents' 39–42
feeling boxes 140
feelings 138–65, *143–7, 149,
    150, 151–6*

angry 26, 70, *156*
bad 141–2, *147, 148, 152,
    164*
confusing (worrying)
    138–40, 157–8, *158,
    159–60*
expressing 70, 141–2
'feeling boxes' 140–1
good feelings 142, *146,
    147, 163*
sad 148, *149*
scared 8, 99, 151, *151,
    153–4*
'yukky' 140–1, 150, *150,
    152*
'female offender' myths 44
feminist movement 40
'fingerprint' worksheet *113*
fitness programs 57
foster parents, fears of 28
friends, saying 'no' to 92

genitals
    names for 6, 40
    see also body privacy
        training
good feelings 142, *146, 147,
    163*
good touches *175–6, 180–2,
    180–2*, 184
'goodness' issues 5, 138
group work 59
groups, risks within 7–8
'gut feelings' 66

hate feelings 26
'hazards' training 96–103
    developing safety
        consciousness 96–9
    emergency procedure
        100–2, *101*
    work cards 102–3
health subjects, integrating
    safety into 200
hearing impediments *see*
    deaf children
help for victims 44

helping services 62
hints about abuse 14–15
'home alone' example 161, *161*
home safety 97, 98, 102, 103
homosexual issues 23, 69–70
hugging 177–9, *177, 178, 179*, 188

'I' statements 91
incident report forms 73
independence development 55–8
independence of therapists 72–3
information needs
    child protection services 69
    children's 5–7, 11–12, 40
information sessions for parents 31–8
    content 36–8
    invitations 31–4
    preparation 34–6
institutions, responsibilities 27–8
integrated approach *see* curriculum development
intellectually disabled children 17–18, 51–2, 58

judging adult motives 5, 20–1, 51, 168
juvenile offenders 67

'Keeping Ourselves Safe' 13, 29–30, 41
'Kidscape' 4
kissing 129, 137, 188
knowledge
    checking parents' 43, 46
    children's need for 5–7, 11–12, 40

language subjects, integrating safety into 200
learning environments, positive 61–2
letters, examples of invitations to parents 31–4
libraries for parents 46
life skills development 55, 58

'making up stories' fears 41, 43
maths subjects, integrating safety into 200
'Me' activities 78, 79, *80–9*
mechanical aids, inappropriate touching 104
meetings for parents
    introductory 31–8
    workshops for parents 42–8
'middle-class' myths 45
mouths, as private body parts 122, 129–30
music subjects, integrating safety into 200

names for body parts 6, 40, 124, 131, 132
National Committee for Prevention of Child Abuse (USA) 46
New Zealand, child protection programs 4, 8, 10, 31
    'Keeping Ourselves Safe' 13, 29–30, 41
'No' *see* assertiveness training
'No-Go-Tell' kit 201
non-verbal children 17–18, 24, 54, 66, 123
    shortage of therapists 72

obedience issues 5, 41–2, 94–5, 138
objectives of parent participation 36
'offender' myths 37, 44
'one-off event' myth 43
open questioning of victims 67
oral deaf children 24
over-protection 57–8
    see also independence

pace of learning 58–61
parental participation 10–11, 13, 14, 15, 29–48
    getting interest 31–8
    handling concerns 39–42
    need for support 38
    preparation 29–31
    workshops 42–8
parents, supporting non-offending 68
peer group risks 7–8
peer tutoring 78
penises
    names for 6
    privacy training 131
personal public disclosures 61–2
personal safety programs *see* child protection programs
physically disabled children 54
    'safety' myth 45
police involvement 67
pornography exposure 16
positive feedback sessions 78
positive learning environments 61–2
powerlessness 5, 10, 55
    disabled children 18, 26, 45, 71
previous experience of abuse 51
privacy needs 56, 57

privacy training *see* body privacy training
problem-solving skill development 59–60
Protective Behaviours Program 13
puppets 59–60, 137, 141, 171

questioning victims 67
questionnaire, for parents' workshops 43–5

Rape Crisis Centre, America 3
'rape blame' myth 44
relationship skill development 55
reporting abuse 20–1
    accidental 61–2
    'exaggeration' myth 42
    ignoring disclosure 22–3
    reasons for not 37–8
    responding to disclosures 23, 46, 65–73
    skills teaching 14–15, *165*, 172–3, 196–8, *199*
'responsibilities' issues 40, 57, 71, 79, 91
return slips, parents' workshops 33
rights, children's 79, 90
risk of abuse *see* vulnerability
role plays 63–4, 98, 141, 185
    deaf children 53

sad feelings 148, *149*
'Safe and Okay' kit 201
safety concepts, introducing parents to 46
safety skills training *see* 'hazards' training
scared feelings 8, 99, 139, 151, *151*, 153–4
school–home communications 31–4

school safety 96–7, 98, 103
secrecy 9–10, 37–8, 46
    disclosing bad secrets 66, 67, 196–8, *199*
'seduction by child' myth 43
self-care 49, 56–8
self-development curriculum 55
self-esteem development 11, 54–5, 56–7, 61, 77–89
    activities 77–9, *80–8*, 89
    deaf children 25
self-protection learning, integrated approach 49–50
severe physical disabilities, children with 54
sex education 21–2, 123, 131, 168
    'appropriate age' fears 40
sexism, acceptance of abuse reports 23
'sexual abuse' definition 36
sexual curiosity, children's 5, 16
sexual touches 190–4
sexuality
    adults' 30, 42
    children's 5–7, 21, 22
shadows, fears of 162
signing deaf children 24
social awareness development 58
social environments, disabled children 18
social studies, integrating safety into 200
songs, body awareness 114–15
staffing arrangements, residential settings 19
stigmatization problems 26
stories, as teaching method 94, 96, 97, 129–30
strangers, identifying dangerous 8–9, 37, 47, 103
support
    by parents 48

for abused children 68–73
for non-offending parents 68
suspected abuse, responding to 65–73

taboos, adults' 5–7, 30
taste, and feelings 148
teachers 22–3, 28, 30
    preparation for safety programs 29–31
teaching methods 12–13, 62–4
    see also brainstorming; role plays; stories; what if cards; worksheets
'teenage seduction' myth 43
telephone calls
    making emergency 62, 91, 100, *101*
    rules for answering home 99
testicles, privacy training 131
therapists
    need for independent 72–3
    shortage of 71–2
therapy, for victims 44, 69–73
    barriers 70–3
third-party approach to problem solving 59–60
tickling 183
'Touch Continuum' 3
touching 10–11, 13, 48, 166–99, *170*
    deaf community norms 53
    different kinds 174–84, *175–84*
    disabled children's disadvantages 19–21, *19–20*, 24, 57
    good *175–6*, 180–2, *180–2*, 184
    painful 185–6

rules for 170–1, 195
    sexual 190–4
    teaching methods 169–73
    worrying 168, 189, *189*
    'yukky' 187–9, *187, 188,*
        189
    see also body privacy
        training
trickery concept 95
'trust' issues 5, 20, 39, 40–1,
    99

UK, child protection
    programs 4
'uncomfortable adults' 30,
    42
University of Alberta Abuse
    and Disability project
    20
USA, child protection
    programs 3–4, 14, 31,
    39

vaginas, privacy training
    about 131
'victim' myths 37, 44
visual impairments,
    children with 54
vulnerability of children 4–8
    dangerous strangers 8–9
    disabled children 17–27,
        19–20
vulvas, privacy training 131

'weak moment' myth 43
'What if...' cards 94, 102–3,
    122–3, 137, 172
'wheelchair safety' myth 45
worksheets
    body awareness *113, 117,*
        119
    developing self-esteem
        79, *80–9*
    feelings *144–5, 146, 147,*
        152–6, 159–60, 163–4
    touching *175–6, 199*

workshops for parents 42–8
    attitudes and
        misconceptions 43,
        45
    facts and myths 43–5
    improving support for
        children 45–8
worrying (confusing)
    feelings 138–40, 157–8,
        158, 159–60
    and touching 168, 189, *189*

'yukky' feelings 140–1, 150,
    150, 152
    and touching 187–9, *187,*
        188, 189

Author Index

Adams, C. 11
Ammerman, R.T. 25
Anderson, C. 3, 51, 63

Bagley, C. 11
Berliner, L. 20
Berrick, J. 14, 15, 31, 45
Blomberg, P.S. 21
Briggs, F.
    and Hawkins 1993 5, 9, 47
    and Hawkins 1994 4, 8,
        11, 12, 13, 22, 23
    1987 14, 31, 56
    1991 4, 5, 6, 9, 10, 13, 15,
        23, 30, 31, 41, 47,
        104, 138
    1994 5, 7, 8, 11, 42
Brown, H. 21
Budin, L.E. 12

Chamberlain, A. 17
Conte, J.R. 13, 20
Cook, M. 5, 7, 8
Craft, A. 21

Downer, A. 13

Farley, S.L. 3
Fenton, M. 55
Fetterman, R.J. 18, 28, 54
Finkelhor, D. 4, 12, 13, 14,
    20, 31, 39
Forchuk, C. 21

Garbarino, J. 20, 26, 44
Gilbert, N. 13
Gochenour, C. 18
Goldman, R. and J. 6, 43
Goodman, L. 21

Hard, S. 21, 23, 104
Hawkins, R.M.
    and Briggs, F. 1993 5, 9, 47
    and Briggs, F. 1994 4, 8,
        11, 12, 13, 22, 23
Howells, K. 5, 7, 8
Hughes, P. 55
Hunter, M. 8

Johnson, C.F. 12

Kennedy, A.E.C. 25
Kennedy, M. 18, 24, 26, 54,
    72
King, K. 11
Kraizer, S.K. 168
Krivacska, J.J. 4, 21

La Fleche, E. 18
Longo, R.E. 18

MacFarlane, K. 11
Mansell, 21
Mayes, G.M. 7, 11, 13, 14, 31
Meadow, K.P. 50
Mindel, E.D. 50
Mitchell, L.K. 22
Moglia, R. 21
Monat-Haller, R. 21
Moore, D.F. 23
Mounty, J.L. 18, 28, 54
Musick, J.L. 21

PACER (Parent Advocacy
    Coalition for
    Educational Rights) 20,
    22

Phoenix, S. 24
Piaget, J. 5
Plummer, C.A. 3, 41

RADAR 56
Rose, L. 21
Ryan, G. 25

Sanford, T.L. 52
Sank, C. 18
Saslawsky, D.A. 13
Schroeder, C. 29
Sengstock, W.L. 21
Senn, C.Y. 17, 18, 19, 21, 22,
    23
Sobsey, D. 20, 21, 22, 25
Strapko, I.M. 4, 13, 39
Sullivan, P.M. 18, 52

Tobin, P. 3

Valtin, R. 10
Vergason, G.A. 21
Vernon, M. 50

Waterman, J. 11
Watson, A.J. 10, 17
Wurtele, S.K. 6, 12, 13, 18, 41

Lightning Source UK Ltd.
Milton Keynes UK
UKOW01f1846031113

9 781853 022456